Miracles of Answered Prayer

MIRACLES OF ANSWERED PRAYER

HIS MYSTERIOUS WAYS

Atworth, Wiltshire

This anglicised edition, © 2005 Eagle Publishing Ltd, Unit 2, Bath Road, Atworth Business Park, Atworth, Wiltshire, SN12 8SB.

Original edition © Ideals Publications, a division of Guideposts. Stories reprinted from Guideposts Magazine, Carmel, NY 10512. Published under the title His Mysterious Ways: Miracles of Prayer.

British Library Cataloguing in Publication Data. A catalogue record for this book is available from the British Library.

Typeset by Eagle Publishing Ltd
Printed by Cox & Wyman Ltd
ISBN No: 0 86347 619 8

Contents

THE UNSEEN PROTECTOR		11
One More Step	Thelma Leavy	13
A Timely Arrival	Pat Hrabe Wehrli	15
A Nagging Feeling	Clara Wallace Nail	17
A Quiet Stretch	Helen Lewis Coffer	19
The Shoes I'm Glad I Forgot	Elizabeth Sherrill	21
An Unseen Protector	Ron Chambers	23
An Unexpected Rescue	Deborah Rose	25
Right Place at the Right Time	Lynn B. Link	27
An Obsolete Fixture	Leonard LeSourd	29
Instructions from Above	David Moore	31
A Mysterious Pounding	Mary Ruth Howes	33
Honking All the Way Home	Elisa Collins	35
A Holy Rock	Robert M. Barr	37
Sweaters for the Boys	Becky Alexander	39
My Spot the Bed	Irene Locker	41
The Message I Couldn't Ignore	Patti Bohlman	43
UNEXPECTED GIFTS		45
A Gift of Laces	Brenda Minner	47
An Unexpected Greeting	Carolyn Hyden	49
A Basketful of Thoughtfulness	Dris Kerr	51
A Lodge Ring for Dad	Mary Sherman Hilbert	53
The Check on the Floor	Sandy Hill	55

A Family Tradition | Cheryl Morrison | 57
A Key for the Lock | Mrs Theo Hill | 59
Baby Shoes for My Sister | Janice Christopher | 61
The Sample Box | Shirley Pope Waite | 63

THE MAGNANIMOUS PROVIDER | 65
My Refresher Course | Jamie van Buskirk | 67
Sunday's Best | Karen Wingate | 69
A Rose on the Fifth Day | Jim Meeker | 71
Road Signs to Guide Us | Marlene Wiechman | 73
One into Ten | Esther McIntosh | 75
An Erratic Old Washing Machine | Annette Sims | 77
The Language I Know | Rosemary Jackson | 79
A Bolt out of the Blue | Duane L. Burch | 81
No Food in the House | Adele Hooker | 83
A Scrawny Mutt Named Buck | Joy Thames | 85
In the Midst of a Storm | Joan Shelton | 87
The Key on the Canned Ham | Helen S. McCutcheon | 89
No Time to Look | Sally Waltman | 91
God Showed Me | Derek Best | 93

MIRACULOUS HEALING | 95
An Unburdened Mind | David Snitker | 97
A Matter of Trust | Joanna Daniel | 99
A Heartfelt Prayer | Ellen St John Barnwell | 101
The Ruby Light | Eros M. Savage | 103
Praying for an Egg | Josephine M. Kuntz | 105
Please Keep Me Safe | Kristina Seidel | 107
Locked in to Think | Doug Jennings | 109
Vision Restored | Don Bell | 111
A Runaway Bus | Evelyn McKay | 113

MYSTERIOUS STRANGERS 115
Then He Vanished — Euphie Eallonardo — 117
No Footprints Left Behind — M. M. McIntosh — 119
A Black Labrador on the Porch — Rev. John E. Troncale — 121
Footprints to Follow — Sandy Seltzer — 123
Swallowed by the Fog — Mary Pettit Holmes — 125
An All-Powerfull Light — Muriel S. Hurst — 127
My Driving Companion — Dorothy Howard — 129
The Kindness of Strangers — Cheryl Toth — 131

THE EVER-PRESENT COMFORTER 133
A Name with Meaning — Rhonda Vecera Naylor — 135
Words of Comfort — Nancy Bayless — 137
When Hearts Appear — Sue Monk Kidd — 139
A Tiny Bud Vase — Charlotte Doty — 141
A Comforting Rain — Sara Snipes — 143
His Name Was Bakht Singh — Edward A. Elliott — 145
A Concert to Heal — Eugenia Eason — 147
Found in the Right Place — Paul Heller — 149
Not a Deer in Sight — Bob Rawlins — 151
The Name on the Pew — Irma Levesque — 153
A Lesson I'll Carry Always — Tim Rich — 155
My Wake-Up Call — Marilyn Teets — 157
Sustained by Words — Margaret Murray — 159
Heavenly Music — Marian T Scheirman — 161
A Love of Daisies — Haven Conner — 163
His Last Words — Faye Field — 165
An Unmistakable Urge — Marion Bond West — 167
Lillian Layton's Daughter — Myrtle 'Cookie' Potter — 169

GLORIOUS WONDERS 171
Release Me — Lloyd B. Wilhide — 173

Radio Rescue	Thomas Coverdale	175
A Valuable Dream	Mary LaMagna Rocco	177
A Fortuitous Phone Call	Mary Anne Hulford	179
The Name on the Mailbox	Virginia Cottrell	181
A Saving Sign	Dorothy Nicholas	183
Her Cry of Glory	Jeanne M. Dams	185
The Correct Phone Number	Edith M. Dean	187
A Field of Cows	Elly Derr	189
A Stunning Blue-White Light	Charles Kaelin Jr MD	191
The Phone that Worked	Orpha E. Abesamis	193
A Bible Found	Charles Sweitzer	195
The Unseen Photographer	Kathy Pierce	197
Sam, AKA Gus	Nancy Rose	199
Elizabeth's Card	Jill Renich-Meyers	201
A Silver Case	Dina Donohue	203

Foreword

The first time I worked with an author on a "His Mysterious Ways" column, I had been at Guideposts for more than a year - the minimum time then editor-in-chief Van Varner required before allowing an editor to work on the magazine's most popular feature. I was surprised by what he told me: "The story should speak for itself without a lot of religious explanation." Van said this with a frown, as if he knew the mayhem a young, inexperienced editor might wreak upon his beloved monthly column.

Fifteen years later "His Mysterious Ways" is still our readers' overwhelming favourite, and I'm finally beginning to understand what Van meant. Each and every one of these short narratives has an incredible true story to tell - of unspoken prayers answered, unknown yearnings realised, and unexpected healings received. Each is a revelation of a divine hand at work in our daily lives, often in ways we never dreamed - until they happen to us.

Indeed these stories do speak for themselves, which is why you need to hear no further from me.

Edward Grinnan
Editor-in-Chief, Guideposts

The Unseen Protector

Hear me when I call. O God . . . have mercy upon me, and hear my prayer.

Psalm 4:1

One More Step

Thelma Leavy

I have always loved the snow. I'm eighty-five and legally blind, but I can see light and some shapes - and I still get excited by fluffy flakes. That's why I ventured out late one snowy afternoon last winter.

I shuffled down my long driveway to my favourite Douglas fir. I went from tree to tree, shaking snow from the boughs. Soon I noticed that I was surrounded by vague and unfamiliar shapes. I'd gone too far into the woods! I turned and started walking back toward my driveway. But which way had I come? Everything was so white - and cold.

The snow fell harder. Wiping tears from my eyes, I rushed forward in a panic. "God," I cried, "please help me."

Abruptly I stopped in my tracks.

I stood perfectly still as a feeling of relief broke through my fear. Then I turned completely around and struck out in a new direction. Finally I came to a fence. It was my boundary line! I followed that fence, just hung to it, until I reached my gate. "Thank you, God," I said.

The next morning, Dan, the young man who shovels snow for me, rushed in; he was alarmed by the footsteps he had seen on the snow-covered property. "Don't worry," I quickly explained, "They're mind."

"Mrs Leavy," Dan said, "I followed those footsteps. They lead up to the edge of the riverbank, right to where the drop-off is steepest. If you'd taken even one more step forward . . ."

But that was where I had stopped and called out - to the one who always leads in the right direction.

A Timely Arrival

Pat Hrabe Wehrli

My five-year-old son and I were driving the lonely ten-mile stretch from town to our home when we hit a bump and heard the thump-thump of a flat tyre.

I began digging our tools from the trunk and discovered we had to tyre iron. There I was, a very pregnant young woman, standing beside a crippled car with a child in the front seat.

In the past year, several local women had been brutally murdered, and the authorities had no idea who the killer was. When a man in a pickup stopped to ask if I needed help, I felt only fear.

"That's all right," I said. "My husband is on his way." In fact, my husband, Gerald, wouldn't be coming along this road for at least another hour.

To my relief, the man drove off. I looked at the distant houses along the highway and tried to decide what to do.

Minutes later, I saw the stranger coming back our way. He stopped on the other side of the highway and slowly walked toward us. "Dear Lord," I prayed, "protect my children."

Just as the man reached us, Gerald pulled up. "There's my husband now," I said, surprised to see that he had left work early. Gerald parked and glanced at the stranger, who left in a hurry.

More than a year later, an area resident confessed to the unsolved murders. As a reserve officer for the county sheriff's department, Gerald escorted the prisoner from the county jail to the mental health centre.

The instant he saw the suspect, Gerald recognised him. It was the stranger who had stopped by my car.

The Nagging Feeling

Clara Wallace Nail

I awoke that morning feeling that there was something I had to do. As I went over the day's schedule, my mind focused on Lena.

Lena lived alone at the end of our road. Elderly and ill, she depended on friends to help her. The day before, I had taken her food, but she insisted I didn't need to come back the next day. "I have everything I need right here," she said.

Lena was proud and dignified and I respected her privacy, but all morning long an inner prompting urged me to go see her. I got the children off to school, loaded the washer, and put the breakfast dishes in the sink; but the nagging wouldn't stop. Finally, I headed down the road.

On her porch I called her name. Usually she came to the door, but this time there was no answer. Hearing a sound inside, I tried the doorknob and let myself into a living room filled with smoke.

Lena lay on the sofa, too weak to get up. In front of her was a small coal heater whose door had come off its hinges. Live coals had fallen on the floor, and Lena had tried to smother them with quilts, clothes, and anything she could reach from the sofa. At any moment the coals might have burst into flames. I had arrived just in time.

Later, after the coals were removed and the house was cleared of smoke, Lena seemed unusually calm about her near tragedy. "Weren't you afraid?" I asked her.

"No," she said, "I knew you'd come. I prayed."

A Quiet Stretch

Helene Lewis Coffer

"Lean on the Lord," friends in our prayer group urged us. "His shoulders are broad."

At the time, my husband and I needed a shoulder to lean on. Our business had turned sour, and our savings were dwindling. And, at retirement age, we were scrounging for jobs.

In the midst of all this, my ninety-four-year-old mother experienced a mental and physical breakdown. She was living with my sister in southwestern Arizona, and she required twenty-four care. Now it looked as if she needed to be put into a nursing home.

One Sunday night I prayed about our problems as I drove home alone from my sister's after a week helping with Mom's care. The narrow, two-lane road was heavy with traffic coming from Las Vegas; the headlights were blinding as they shone in my eyes. Three different times I came over hills to find a car coming at me in my lane, and each time, I had to pull off the side of the road to avoid a collision. I was thankful that those broad shoulders were there.

Two weeks later I made the same trip with my husband. In full daylight we reached the road just north of Kingman, Arizona. "This was the stretch," I told him, "where I had to pull off."

We looked and looked, and we grew quieter and quieter.

For that entire forty-mile section of Highway 93, cactus and greasewood and mesquite grew close to the roadside. There were no shoulders on the road - only His to lean on.

The Shows I'm Glad I Forgot

Elizabeth Sherrill

Of all times to have the airline lose my luggage! It was only my toiletries case with my one pair of good shoes, but of all places to wind up without them!

I'd flown out to New Mexico for a one-day seminar sponsored by the Southwest Christian Writers' Association. "No one will care about your shoes," Margaret Cheasebro, the group's president, assured me.

Undoubtedly, Margaret was right, but of all times ... Even as I thought it, a phrase from our church's communion service came to mind: "we should at all times, and in all places, give thanks unto Thee." At all times? I wondered.

At the seminar's close, several writers came up to the stand. Suddenly, there was an ear-splitting crack and the sound of exploding glass. A woman shouted, "Lie down! Everyone!"

Through the window she had seen a man brandishing a gun. Later we learned that he had been drinking and shooting at telephone poles. From the wall behind the speaker's stand, the police recovered the tip of an electric screwdriver fired from a muzzleloading pistol.

While Margaret filled out the police report, the rest of us relived our escape, each recalling a step forward or a second's delay that had kept her out of the line of fire.

For my part, I traced a trajectory from the window to the wall, an inch over the spot where I'd been standing. I was thinking of a pair of two-and-a-half-inch heels in a missing bag. I echoed an ancient prayer: "we should at all times, and in all places, give thanks unto Thee."

An Unseen Protector

Ron Chambers

I was going snorkelling in the Palm Beach inlet with my fourteen-year-old son, Don, and our diving instructor, Jerry. We were to swim out past the jetty, then float into the channel with the tide. I hesitated. The breakers were enormous.

I put on the foam rubber wet-vest and Jerry's weight belt to offset the vest's buoyancy, and we dove in. Jerry and Don paddled along in front, with me right behind. As we swam out, the distance between us grew. Better swim harder, I thought. But I was swimming as hard as I could. Looking ahead, I saw Jerry and Don clear the end of the jetty.

In the next instant, a wave slammed me against the rocks. Then another and another. The barnacles on the boulders slashed my arms and legs. The heavy weight around my waist dragged me down. I tried to grab onto the rocks, but they were too large, too slippery, and too sheer.

Exhausted and battered, I knew right then that I was going to die. I was pleasantly surprised to find that I felt prepared for death. I imagined myself standing in the presence of God, and the thought gave me great peace. I looked up and said quietly, "I'm ready, Father . . ."

Needless to say, I did not die. I'm still mystified by the way in which I was saved. And to this day I'm drawn often to Psalm 27:5: "For in the time of trouble, He shall hide me in His pavilion . . . He shall set me up upon a rock."

In my time of trouble, a huge wave suddenly crashed into the jetty, and a swirling column of water lifted me up six feet in the air, spun me around into a sitting position, and placed me safely on top of a rock.

The Unexpected Rescue

Deborah Rose

Tuesday night was chicken night at the restaurant where I was a waitress, but on this Tuesday few customers ordered it. "Take some home," said the manager. The chicken was greasy, so I wrapped it in plastic and put it in a box and a bag.

The last customers lingered and we closed late. Missing the last bus and unable to afford a cab, I began walking home through the deserted Milwaukee streets. I prayed and sang a hymn. God would see me home safely.

But he didn't. A man with a knife leapt out of the shadows, pushed me down a dark side street, and spoke in ugly language of what he'd do when we reached his place on Brady Street. Why had God forsaken me?

Despite my anger, I kept praying. And then, out of nowhere I heard four words. They were very clear and very firm. "Debbie, eat your chicken." What? Was I losing my mind?

As I was dragged along. I struggled with all the wrappings and pulled out a chicken breast. Crying too hard to eat, I just carried it in my hand. We had reached Brady Street.

Two large dogs rummaged in spilled trash cans along the street. Suddenly, the dogs looked up and sniffed the air. Growling and baring teeth, they charged at us. My attacker fled.

The dogs did not lunge at me. They fixed their eyes on the chicken in my hand. I tore off meat and threw it down, where they fought hungrily for it. Dropping pieces every few yards, I got the stray dogs to follow me home. By the time I was safely inside, I'd begun to understand. Debbie, eat your chicken - the chicken that had been wrapped too thickly to be smelled even by a dog. But in my hand . . .

Right Place at the Right Time

Lynn B. Link

With our four little children and two visiting nieces to tuck in, bedtime that night took a long time. I said a prayer over each drowsy child and asked God to watch over them. Later, when my husband and I went to bed, I floated on the edge of sleep, where I was lulled by the innocent noises drifting down the hallway - deep-sleep sighs and the mumbled words of dreamy conversations.

At 4.30am I woke up abruptly. I heard a niece whimper. Suddenly, I was out of bed and running down the hallway - but not to the room where my niece lay. Without knowing why, I ran to my children's bedroom on the other side of the house.

I stood in their doorway, hearing my heart pounding in my ears. Something bad was about to happen. I could feel it.

Seconds ticked by. The children slept peacefully in their bunk beds. All was so quiet. So why did I run here? Was I dreaming?

Then, right before my very eyes, the upper half of the bunk bed came apart. I rushed forward to catch the heavy mattress board and the mattress before they crashed down onto my littlest one, Rachel, in the bottom bunk. I cried for help and my husband came; in a few moments all was set to rights.

Andy and I stepped back. "Why were you in here?" he asked.

"I don't know."

"Thank God you were," Andy said. And with a smile he added, "Listen, we're whispering, and the kids never even woke up."

An Obsolete Fixture

Leonard E. LeSourd

When our sons Chet and Jeff were teenagers, they always celebrated the end of a long trip home to Florida by dashing out of the car and jumping into our swimming pool. It was the finishing touch to a journey - as much a family tradition as the prayers that started a trip. My wife Catherine, our children, and I never set out without first asking for God's protection from tip's beginning to trip's end.

One year before leaving Virginia, the family prayed together as usual, asking God to be especially close. We made the trip south without incident.

On arriving home, the boys failed to make their customary dash to the pool. "Too tired," they said.

In checking things around the house, I started to switch on the underwater light that creates a beautiful glow in the pool. But the switch was already in the "on" position. That's odd, I thought. I guess the bulb burned out. Then a prickly feeling crept over me.

Immediately I taped the switch in the "off" position and made sure that no one entered the pool.

The next morning I called an electrician, who checked the pool light carefully. "You've got an old, obsolete fixture here," he said.

"Must've been here before you bought the place. Anyway, water got into the light socket and shorted the circuit. It's a good thing nobody went swimming, they would have been electrocuted."

It was more than a good thing. For our family, it was one more example of how God touches our lives in supernatural ways when we seek His help.

Instructions from Above

David Moore

Henry Gardner was flying me to Asheville, North Carolina, in his Cessna 180. We'd taken off from Victoria, Texas, and had stopped in Jackson, Mississippi, to fix a malfunctioning radio.

Now we were nearing Asheville, only to find that the fog was so thick that the controller wouldn't let us land. "Sorry," he said over the radio, "you'd better head to Greenville." But we couldn't.

We didn't have enough fuel to make it to Greenville. "We're going to have to land," Henry insisted, and we were granted permission to make an emergency landing. The radio sputtered a few times and Henry lowered the plane.

"Pull it up!" came a shout. To our horror we saw we were about to land on the interstate! Henry pulled hard on the stick and we barely missed a highway overpass.

"If you listen to me," the voice on the radio said, "I'll show you how to get back in." And then came a series of careful, detailed instructions: "Raise it up." "To your left a little." "Easy, easy." "You're nearing the runway. Let it down - now!"

The lights of the runway suddenly appeared out of the fog. Never had I seen such a welcome sight. We had landed safely.

First we thanked God. Then as soon as we could, we went to

thank the air-traffic controller, who looked at us in bewilderment.

"I don't understand," he said. "I lost contact with you after I told you to make an emergency landing. Your radio sputtered and you were gone."

A Mysterious Pounding

Mary Ruth Howes

When I was growing up, I always liked to hear my father tell the story of a strange premonition he'd had as a young missionary in China. Dad's superior, Mr Sinton, had just left Luchou for an extended journey to outlying missions when Dad was overwhelmed with the feeling that Mr Winton was in mortal danger. Every night, Dad prayed for his safety.

When Mr Sinton returned, he told about having retired one night in a guest house where a tiny charcoal brazier burned. Later that evening Mr Sinton had heard a loud, mysterious pounding. Getting up, he went to the window, pushed it open, and looked out. No one was there. He started toward the door, but the next thing he knew, he was waking up flat on the floor. He had been overcome by toxic fumes from the brazier. Opening that window had saved his life!

Several years ago, when Dad was eighty-two, he called me at the office. "I had such a vivid dream early this morning," he said, "that I had to call you. I dreamed you were in danger. Is your house okay?"

I didn't want to do it, but after remembering Dad's story about Mr Sinton, I went home - only to discover my sick cat sleeping in front of the electric heater. There was no fire. There was no danger.

I turned off the heater and, feeling foolish, returned to the office.

At home that night, I turned on the heater again. Fifteen minutes later the lights in the kitchen flickered and went out. The motor on the heater had burned out, blowing the fuses and filling the kitchen with acrid smoke . . .

Honking all the Way Home

Elisa Collins

I was a missionary kid; I grew up in Comitancillo, a Mayan village in the highlands of Guatemala. My dad was a Bible translator, and my mom was a nurse. One day in February 1993, we drove to Guatemala City to pick up a work team to help us build a library. Unfortunately, we rented a van with a horn that honked every time we hit a bump in the road.

We left early, hoping to get to the village before dark. (It wasn't safe to travel at night.) Three hours into the trip - the horn honking at every pothole - a car swerved in front of us. Two men jumped out and pointed guns at us. They leaped into our van and forced my father to follow a second car.

"No flashing your lights or honking your horn," one said. The horn! I thought, terrified of hitting a bump. How can we control it?

Immediately I started to pray. The men kept demanding money. We didn't let them know that we had $2500 in cash hidden in a briefcase in the back of the van.

The men made us turn onto a steep, bumpy road, where we parked. "Give us the keys to the back," the robbers said. But they couldn't open the door and they were getting nervous. After a few frantic minutes, they threw the keys in the nearby bushes and left with only a few of our personal possessions.

After thanking God for our safety, we retrieved the keys. Dad checked the rear door, and it opened easily for him. Then he backed down the bumpy road. For the first time since the assault, the horn started honking - and it honked all the way home.

A Hole Rock

Robert M. Barr

The rock was bigger than a watermelon. When I uncovered it in the field I was ploughing that November, it was smudged with black earth. In the spring, I came back to move it and discovered that the winter rains and snows had washed it clean.

I stared at the rock. Right on the face of that big, dark boulder, a pink cross stood out, as clear as if it had been chiselled.

"Why, that's the cross of Christ," I said to myself. "This isn't going to a rock pile. It's a holy thing!"

I hauled the rock up to the house to show my wife, Bun, and she felt the same as I did. We thought about God telling the Israelites to keep a sign of their faith written on the doorposts of their houses (Deuteronomy 11:18-20), and we decided to set the rock by our door.

Everybody who saw the rock thought it was unusual - even before the tornado of August 1979. Bun and I could hear the storm in the distance while we watched the news on TV. "Well, folks," the weatherman said, "there's a tornado watch, and my best advice is to keep an eye on the sky."

"I'll just go out and take a look," I told Bun.

And, by golly, that thing was coming right at us - a wide, black funnel cutting through my cornfield and chewing up everything in its path. It was moving southwest to northeast, the way tornados generally do.

Bun and I hid in the cellar and prayed. But our neighbours saw what happened outside.

Not once, but twice, that tornado came right up to our door where the rock with the cross of Christ sat, and each time it backed away!

Sweaters for the Boys

Becky Alexander

Late in World War II, my father was on the battlefront in Germany. In March 1945, while his Canadian regiment awaited supplies, Dad was ordered to Aldershot, England, to be decorated by King George VI.

The weather was raw in Aldershot, but Dad had given his regulation greatcoat to a soldier back at the front. Shivering, he headed straight for the Red Cross centre and picked from the bin of sweaters a thick, hand-knit sweater with a double collar. It fitted perfectly under his tunic and warmed him without his breaking the uniform code.

After receiving the military medal for bravery at Buckingham Palace, Dad rejoined his regiment and was issued another coat. He packed the sweater away in his kit.

Dad returned home safely to Canada in January 1946. His mother was glad to do his laundry again. While sorting his clothes, she held up the sweater in amazement. Then to my father's astonishment, she grabbed a pair of scissors and snipped the collar.

Like many women during the war, Grandma had knit sweaters for the young men overseas. She always put a note and postage money inside so they could write back. "I prayed for the boys who would receive my handiwork and asked God to guide them safely home," she said. Many corresponded with her for years after.

While Grandma's hands had faithfully knitted, other Hands had guided her son safely home. Inside the collar of the sweater was some postage money - and a note she had written to a boy overseas.

My Spot on the Bed

Irene Lockera

Every spring my husband, Morton, and I travel from Los Angeles to visit our family in the South. But last January Morton wasn't feeling up to a long plane ride.

"You go," he said. "Enjoy. I can take care of myself."

In our forty years together, I had never taken a trip without Morty. I called him every night from my niece's house in Nashville. On the morning of my departure, as I was about to leave for the airport, we got news that an earthquake had hit Los Angeles at 5.31 a.m. I tried frantically to get through to Morty.

"God," I asked angrily, "why didn't you nudge me to stay home with him?" "We would have been together, sleeping side by side when the earthquake struck. Instead, Morty had to fend for himself.

I finally reached my son, who assured me that Morty was fine. When I got home, I was never so happy to see him. It didn't matter that almost everything in our apartment was destroyed. The dishwasher had been torn loose and flung through the kitchen wall. In the bedroom, broken bottles, picture frames, and mirrors covered the floor. The highboy was overturned.

My eyes darted o the bed, where Morty had been safe amid the mayhem. I thanked God for watching over him. And then I stared unbelieving at our nineteen-inch, fifty-pound TV set. It had been thrown from the top of the highboy onto the bed - and it had landed exactly on the spot where I would have been sleeping if I had stayed home.

THE MESSAGE I COULDN'T IGNORE

PATTI BOHLMAN

My home was a two-bedroom trailer in rural western Oklahoma, and the winter of 1978 was just beginning when I heard the weather report on television: an ice storm was coming.

I gathered blankets in preparation for the storm, and then, sure enough, the power went out. I said a prayer to ask God to get me safely through the night, and I made myself comfortable on the couch under the blankets.

At midnight I awoke as the television and lights came back on. Feeling all was well, I turned everything off and stumbled to bed.

Fifteen minutes later, I awoke from a sound sleep. A voice was calling me urgently, a voice I always heeded unquestioningly. "Patti, get up," Mother said.

A glow was coming from the kitchen, and I jumped out of bed and ran to see flames shooting from the hot-water tank. I rushed outside. By the time the firemen arrived, the trailer was totally engulfed in flames. Numb with exhaustion, I watched as fire consumed my home.

Other family members arrived from nearby, and we surveyed the ruins. "Thank goodness you got out," my sister said. "What if you hadn't awoken in time?"

It was then that I told the story of how I had been roused by Mother's voice. The others stared at me in disbelief.

Why was it so amazing to think that she had saved my life? Because Mother had passed away in March the year before.

God had sent me a message I could not ignore.

Unexpected Gifts

And the Lord said unto him: I have heard thy prayer and thy supplication that thou has made before . . .

1 Kings 9:3

A Gift of Laces

Brenda Minner

Hurrying through the supermarket, I knocked over a display of shoelaces. In my embarrassment, I flung one packet into the cart; and, after paying, I tossed it into my purse. Then I was off to the rehabilitation hospital where I'd been visiting Donald, a man whose arms and legs were paralyzed after a fall from a ladder.

That day Donald was unusually despondent. "Brenda," he said, "Sometimes I feel God simply doesn't care anymore."

"You know He cares . . ." I began. But I had no real answer for him. So we sat in silence.

"Oh, by the way," Donald said as I started to leave, "the nurse broke one of my shoestrings. Could you get me a new pair?"

I opened my purse and took out the packet from the supermarket. We stared at the shoestrings in amazement, then I laced them into Donald's shoes.

Shoestrings! For a pair of shoes on feet that could not even move to wear them out. For a set of hands that could not even tie the bow.

"Donald, if God cares enough to supply you with shoestrings even before you ask," I said, "I'm certain He cares about you in more important ways."

A smile broke onto his face. "Yes, you're right," Donald said. "I'm sure too."

Shoestrings. Whenever I'm discouraged, I think of them. And then I remember that God cares for me too - right down to the laces in my shoes.

An Unexpected Greeting

Carolyn Hyden

It was Mother's Day, and I was especially worried about Mom this year. For the first time, she would be all alone on the holiday. I kept thinking, if only Gary were with her.

My big brother Gary had been a quiet, caring man who loved helping others. Seven years earlier when my father died, Gary moved in with Mom and took a job at a convenience store nearby.

He was a great comfort to her. They played games together, watched TV, and read books. Then one November evening the store was robbed, and Gary was shot and killed. Afterward Mom's loneliness was acute, and I never left her out of my prayers.

That Mother's Day I called to see how she was. To my surprise, she sounded calm and at peace; then she told me why.

The day before, she had received cards from her five children and seven grandchildren. But walking back from the mailbox, she couldn't help dwelling on the one card she would not be getting, the one child she would never hear from again.

Inside the empty house Mom brewed a cup of tea and reread her cards. Finally she gathered them all together and put them on a bedside shelf for safekeeping. And there on the shelf, she spotted a book she'd long intended to read. As she picked it up and turned the pages, out dropped an old faded greeting card with a handwritten message. It was:

Happy Mother's Day
Love, Gary

A Basketful of Thoughtfulness

Doris Kerr

On Christmas Day my husband, Dick, and I were the first on the scene of an accident - two cars had collided head-on.

As a registered nurse I'd hoped I could help, but it was too late. Dick and I prayed with a teenage boy who was pinned against his seat. We watched him die before the ambulance arrived.

In the days that followed, I managed to locate the boy's parents through the phone book. I spoke to his parents and described what had happened. Through their tears, they expressed gratitude. They had known little of the circumstances of his death and were comforted to know that their son had died while God was close through prayer.

Three months later, on the Saturday before Easter, Dick and I had held hands and prayed together at the kitchen table before he left to go to a men's breakfast. Not long after came a telephone call from the hospital. Dick had suffered a heart attack. I rushed to his bedside but arrived too late to say good-bye.

I was numb. On the way home, I was overwhelmed with grief. I could barely enter the house. I walked into the kitchen where only hours before we had sat next to each other, reading, talking, praying.

There on the table was a basketful of fresh spring flowers - a sign of new birth and a symbol of the Resurrection. I looked at the card to see who could have unknowingly anticipated my need so beautifully.

The gift had come from the parents of the boy who died on Christmas Day - but the comfort was God's.

A Lodge Ring for Dad

Mary Sherman Hilbert

My dad was frugal about some things, and he wouldn't spend much on himself. For instance, although he was devoted to his lodge, he wouldn't indulge in a lodge ring. But his love for his children, especially my brother Bob, was extravagant.

When World War II broke out, my handsome, fearless brother became a Marine fighter pilot. Early in 1944, he died under enemy fire in the South Pacific.

Mother's faith sustained her, but my father aged before our very eyes. He began missing work. He lost interest in things. He even stopped going to his lodge meetings.

As Christmas approached, Mother and I worried more and more about Dad. The holiday had been Bob's favourite; his Christmas surprises were legendary: a doll house made at school for me, a puppy hidden away for his little brother, an expensive dress for Mother bought with the first money Bob ever earned.

Dad's grief continued to drain his strength. Mother and I prayed together, "Dear God, help us through Christmas."

On December 23rd, an official-looking package from the government arrived; it contained more of Bob's personal effects. Dad watched grimly as Mother unwrapped Bob's dress uniform. As she refolded it to pack it away, she automatically went through the pockets.

"What's this?" she murmured suddenly. Then, with a little cry, she handed it to Dad.

I'll never forget the look that transformed his face into a blend of wonder, hope, and healing, as if Bob were still with us.

In his hand, he held a neatly folded fifty-dollar bill with a note in Bob's handwriting: for Dad's lodge ring.

THE CHEQUE ON THE FLOOR

SANDY HILL

When it came time to renew my subscription to a magazine, I sent a cheque. The next month I received a notice telling me that I hadn't paid. I immediately sent a copy of my cheque, accompanied by a letter of explanation. Thinking the matter was resolved, I stuffed the cheque into a folder full of other receipts.

Later, I was annoyed to find a notice in the mail at work from a collection agency for the amount owed on the subscription.

"But I have paid!" I stormed, "What do I do now?"

A co-worker suggested, "Turn it over to the Lord."

I didn't think the Lord was that interested in my daily life. Still, right there at my workstation I prayed, "Lord, it's just a little thing. But I could use your help."

That night I asked my husband, Danny, to help me unearth that cancelled cheque. We searched through our voluminous files - without success.

I stomped down to the basement to put some laundry in the dryer. As I reached the bottom step, I spotted an envelope on the floor. I knew it hadn't been there when I had come down before supper. And I had been the only one in the basement all evening. I opened the envelope and gasped.

I ran upstairs yelling, “Danny, the cheque! It was on the basement floor. In an envelope.” His mouth dropped open with surprise.

I mailed off another copy of the cheque with a letter to the collection agency, and that was the end of that. But a new relationship with God was just beginning.

A Family Tradition

Cheryl Morrison

"No hot chocolate on Christmas Eve?" our teenage daughter, Christine, asked. I looked away.

"Next year," I promised as she went to get ready for the midnight service.

We had always had hot chocolate on Christmas Eve; it was a tradition. This year we couldn't afford even that simple item. When my husband, Jack, was laid off six months earlier, he started a claims-adjusting business and worked out of our basement; but the response had been dreadful. Then, to add to our woes, our car's transmission died.

Our older daughter, Janice, contributed her earnings from her first full-time job, and the girls never complained about doing without. Still, as the year drew to a close, our financial picture looked bleaker and bleaker.

As we headed out the door, my eyes fell on our old artificial tree draped with last year's dulled tinsel. I couldn't even squeeze money for hot chocolate out of our budget, I thought. During the service, I prayed silently, "Oh, Lord, you promised to take care of us. Have you forgotten?"

Everyone except me was uplifted by the message of hope in the service. At its close, people hugged and shook hands.

As we bundled up in coats and scarves, Christine's youth counsellor called to us, "Wait!" She pulled a ribboned jar from her bag. "Merry Christmas," she said as she handed us hot chocolate mix!

She hadn't known about our family tradition. And she didn't know that, to me, this simple gift was a reminder that God had not forgotten us after all.

A Key for the Lock

Mrs Theo Hill

It was a cold and windy midwinter day, but I was busy - and warm - inside the house I had lived in alone for the past fifteen years. I needed some wrapping paper, so I pulled down the folding stairs and started climbing to the attic. I was eighty-one at the time; and the moment the frigid attic air hit me, I knew I should have put on a coat. Oh well, I thought, I'd hurry.

To keep the warm air downstairs, I shut the door to the attic storage room behind me. I heard a click. I knew immediately that I was locked in. The door had no knob, I'd taken it off to replace a broken one downstairs. And there was no one else in the house.

The cold penetrated my bones. I wrapped myself in a blanket to stop my shaking and looked out the attic window. No neighbours were in sight. And the window was stuck shut from years of disuse.

An hour passed and then another. "Dear Lord, please send my children to help me," I prayed. I knew this was unrealistic. None of my four children was due to visit.

At my feet sat a yellowed and dusty pile of my son Billy's school papers. On top of them lay an old pencil. I picked it up and thought of the hours it had spent in Billy's hand.

Once again I prayed. As clear as any words I'd ever heard, a question came to me, What is that in thy hand?

I looked at the pencil and my glance fell not on the leaded end, but on the metal end that had once held an eraser. It was now flattened, no doubt by my Billy's biting down as he sought to unlock a math problem.

I went to the door and inserted this end of the pencil into the keyhole. The lock turned. The door opened.

Baby Shoes for my Sister

Janice Christopher

It was time for a new pair of shoes for my baby sister, Connie, so Mama took the four of us kids to the shoe store. Scanning the shelves, she stopped in front of a tiny pair of high-top shoes.

"These are exactly what Connie needs," she said, running her fingers over the smooth, soft, white leather. Then Mama looked at the price tag and sighed. "I don't think we can afford them," she said.

What now? Mama sat and bowed her head. After a few minutes she stood and led us out of the store. "Don't worry," she told us. "Everything will work out somehow."

I stroked Connie's brown curls, hoping Mama was right. My little sister couldn't go to church barefoot the next day.

When we got home I scrambled out of the car and up the path. I saw Mama stop and stare, astonishment blooming on her face. What was she looking at? Then I noticed.

Dangling from the doorknob was the prettiest pair of baby shoes I ever saw. They were made of white top-grain leather and looked as if they had never been worn. I helped Mama put them on my sister's feet. They were a perfect fit!

After church the next day, our neighbour came up to us. "I'm so glad you could use those shoes," she said. "My grand-daughter outgrew them before she even had a chance to wear them."

So that's where they came from, I thought. Holding Connie's hand as she put one foot in front of the other, I knew who had really given us the shoes.

The Sample Box

Shirley Pope Waite

Two months after my husband finished graduate school and started a new job, I gave birth to our first child. We had very little money and at times we had none at all.

The days went by and I eked out this and that. One morning after I'd gathered up the baby's laundry, I found I'd run out of detergent. Our monthly pay cheque wasn't due till the end of the week, and we barely had enough money left for our food needs, never mind soap. But I had to have clean diapers for my baby! It was one of those little frustrations that wells up to blimp-size discouragement.

"Oh, Lord, You know I need soap. I pray that my folks send me money - soon." My parents periodically sent a small cheque. They were the only source I could think of.

I heard a noise at the door. Could it be the mail carrier? Somehow I actually expected God would answer me that quickly. I glanced out the window, but no mailman. It must have been the wind rattling the screen.

I went on with my housework. I kept crying out to the Lord. "What will I do about these diapers? Oh, Lord, what will I do?"

I suddenly felt prompted to go to the front door. Perhaps the mail carrier had come and I'd missed seeing him. Perhaps a cheque . . .

I opened the door, and hanging on the handle was a plastic sack containing a sample box of a new detergent!

What did I learn about prayer that day! That God not only answers prayers, but He has His own way of chiding a frantic housewife. As Isaiah 65:24 reads. ". . . before they call, I will answer, and while they are yet speaking, I will hear."

The Generous Provider

And all things, whatsoever ye shall ask in prayer, believing, ye shall receive.

Matthew 21:22

My Refresher Course

Jamie Van Buskirk

Sophomore year of high school wasn't easy. One night as I got into bed worrying about the next day's work, I prayed, "Prepare me for tomorrow."

I couldn't sleep. I tossed and turned under the covers, and I finally snapped the lamp back on. I thumbed through an old yearbook, then picked up a magazine.

Still restless, I reached for something else and found the emergency medical manual for a course I had taken two years earlier. Boring, I thought. If anything will put me to sleep, this will., I had forgotten the finer points, but one emergency procedure in particular came back to me as I read. When I finished, I let the manual drop to the floor, and I fell sound asleep.

In the hallway at school the next morning, I yawned as I glanced into the biology classroom. The teacher was sprawled on the floor. "Mr Heuschkel?" I asked as I walked in.

His face was almost purple. I dropped down and put my ear to his face. He wasn't breathing. "Call 911!" I yelled.

The instructions for CPR were fresh in my mind. I gave him a break and checked again. Nothing. I couldn't find a pulse either. I repeated the steps, working alone until the chemistry teacher rushed in and took over cardiac compression while I continued mouth-to-mouth resuscitation. By the time paramedics took Mr Heuschkel to the hospital, his pulse was back to normal.

"Did a CPR class prepare you for this?" my principal asked.

"Yes," I answered. But the night before, God had given me a refresher course.

Sunday's Best

Karen Wingate

Right before I left Arizona for my first year of college in Ohio, my mom cooked my favourite meal: oven-fried chicken, aubergine sautéed with onions and tomatoes, and homemade whole-wheat bread.

The initial week at school was hectic; I had to learn my way around campus and find all my classes. For the first time I my life, I had to budget my time and money.

When Sunday rolled around, I was looking forward to a break. The school cafeteria was closed so I thought |I would go out to dinner. After church I checked my wallet. Only a single dollar bill was tucked inside. How did I goof up? I wondered. I wanted to call my mom and dad, but I didn't want to worry them.

As I returned to my dorm room, a swell of homesickness swept over me. I remembered the dinner my mom had cooked before I left. I had always taken my next meal for granted, but now I had no food, no family nearby, and no money. "Give us this day our daily bread," I prayed, fighting off tears.

Again, I searched my wallet. This time instead of money, I found a piece of paper with a phone number that a friend back home had given me. "My parents live in Cincinnati," he had said. "They'd love to meet you. Call them." I did.

"We're just about to sit down to Sunday dinner," Mrs Ensign said. "Come right over."

The Lord looked out for me that day. Mrs Ensign's menu was out of this world: oven-fried chicken, aubergine sautéed with onions and tomatoes, and homemade whole-wheat bread!

A Rose on the Fifth Day

Jim Meeker

It was a grey February afternoon, but I was thinking of flowers. I was on my way to my daughter's birthday celebrations, and I wanted to take her a bouquet. She lived near Pittston, Pennsylvania, about thirty miles from my home. I searched without success for a florist before spotting a mom-and-pop grocery store. They will know, I thought.

An elderly woman was coming out of the store as I pulled over. When I asked about a florist, she had a surprising reaction. Her eyes brightened and a smile brought a blush to her cheeks. "Flowers?" she asked. "Someone's getting flowers today?"

"Yes. It's my daughter's birthday."

The old woman directed me to a nearby florist. I tried to thank her, but she turned quickly and walked away.

I purchased a colourful bouquet for my daughter at the shop. I also decided to take a remembrance to the woman who led me there - an exquisite red rose.

I drove back to the grocery store, and the clerk behind the counter nodded when IU described the old woman. "She comes in nearly every day," she said.

"Would you give her this?" I asked.

"A rose!" said the woman with excitement. "She's been saying a special prayer for five days and today is the fifth day!"

"What does that have to do with the rose?"

"It's a message from God," she explained. "She told me that if she received a rose on the fifth day, God had answered her prayer."

ROAD SIGNS TO GUIDE US

MARLENE WIECHMAN

Coming back from a vacation trip, my family and I were driving along a desolate stretchy of highway in Wyoming when our daughter, Emily, who was almost five, suddenly said she felt sick.

Right away I knew something was terribly wrong. Her eyes kept shifting; and when I coaxed her, she would briefly bring them back into focus. "Emily!" I called to her. And then she lost consciousness.

"Lord," I prayed. "we need to get her to a doctor, fast." The nearest town was Rock Springs, about sixty miles away Every minute was precious. Emily had suffered a stroke when she was seven months old, and we were always on the alert for any signs of another one.

At last we were nearing Rock Springs. But once there, how would we find a doctor? To our relief, we spotted a blue sign with a white H on it. And soon after that, another sign, then another directed us to the hospital, where Emily was ushered into the emergency room. Soon her condition stabilised, and she improved rapidly. A mild epileptic seizure, the doctor said.

That afternoon my husband and my father drove out to the highway to a gas station we'd seen, and they got lost coming back to the hospital. They had been counting on the hospital signs to guide them. When they told the doctor of their misadventure, he said, "What signs? There are no hospital signs on that road."

And yet we had seen those signs - just when they were needed most.

One into Ten

Esther McIntosh

I had only two one-dollar bills in my wallet; and they had to last until payday, ten days away. My husband was away on business, and I was at home with our two children, conserving every cent.

On Monday my father called to say he needed to attend a union meeting on Friday afternoon. Would I come and stay with Mother? She was bedridden with brain cancer and had to have someone help her with her medicine. I didn't hesitate to say yes. Back in 1970, one dollar would buy enough gas to get there and back, and I would still have an "emergency" dollar left.

All week long my five-year-old kept asking for a treat from the ice cream truck. And each time, I would open my wallet, show her the two one-dollar bills, and explain why we couldn't afford such a luxury.

When we arrived on Friday, Daddy's parting words were, "Don't forget to give Mom her Dilantin," her anticonvulsant medicine. After he'd gone, I discovered that the bottle was empty. I was terrified that Mother would go into convulsions if she didn't get her medicine on time.

Mother told me to check her purse and a couple of other places for loose change, but that was all I found - loose change. I telephoned my sisters, but no one was home. The prescription cost over eight dollars. Where would I get the money?

"God will take care of it," Mother said.

At my wit's end, I decided to go to the pharmacist's with my lone dollar and beg him to trust me for the rest. When I looked in my wallet again, I was stunned.

That single was a ten-dollar bill.

An Erratic Old Washing Machine

Annette Sims

In 1968 my husband, Billy, was about to go to Vietnam, leaving me with a three-year-old, a second child on the way, and an erratic old washing machine. Every morning the machine would stop dead after the wash cycle, its tub full of soapy, undrained water.

Billy had a way of fixing the machine; he would take the top off and jiggle a wire. But what would we do when Billy went away? I prayed for Billy's safe return to us, and I didn't think about the washing machine until the day after he left.

That morning I reluctantly filled the machine with dirty clothes and said, "Lord, what am I going to do with a three-year-old, a new baby, and a busted washer? Please, God, help me through this."

An hour later I returned to the machine and, to my amazement, the clothes had gone through a complete wash and rinse, and they were now ready for the dryer. For days after that the washer continued to work perfectly. Soon I forgot the problem altogether.

In January 1969, Billy came safely home. He brought a duffel bag of dirty clothes. That very day I threw them into the machine and quickly returned to the living room to be with Billy as he got to know our new son.

An hour later I went back to the washing machine. Can you guess what I found?

Soapy, undrained water!

I could only laugh and feel more blessed than ever. Billy was home and the washer was back to its old dirty tricks!

The Language I Know

Rosemary Jackson

I volunteer at a soup kitchen in Santa Fe where you are as likely to hear Spanish as English. Many times I've wished I could speak Spanish, especially with two of my favourite regulars, whom I'll call Juan and Miguel. Luckily Juan's English is good enough that he can translate for Miguel, who speaks none at all.

"Hey, how's it going?" I asked them one day.

Juan told me he and Miguel had been looking everywhere for work. "No luck," he said. They'd run out of money and were sleeping in a nearby park. I could only imagine how tough it was to find work, especially when you are homeless.

"Why don't we pray about it?" I suggested and waited for Juan to translate for Miguel. Then we all held hands and asked God to help them find jobs.

After that I didn't see Juan and Miguel for a while. I figured they might have had to go out of town to find work. Then one day they were back.

"We want to thank you," Juan said. Miguel smiled and spoke in Spanish as his friend translated for him: "Miguel says, 'Prayer really works. We both have jobs!'"

"Let's give thanks," I urged. I bowed my head and said a short prayer of thanksgiving aloud. After saying "Amen," I opened my eyes to find my friends staring at me.

Miguel spoke in an urgent tone, then Juan explained for me. "My friend says and I say it too. That was a beautiful prayer. Thank you. Your Spanish is flawless."

Flawless? I don't see how. For I had said that prayer in English, the only language I know.

A Bolt Out of the Blue

Duane L. Burch

We were about thirty miles away from the Marine barracks in Fort Meade, Maryland, where my friend and I were stationed, when the dashboard warning lights came on and the engine sputtered. Fortunately, we were able to make it to an emergency pull-off area. But we were due back in an hour and a half, after which time we would be considered AWOL.

I poked around under the hood and discovered that a bolt holding the generator in place had worked its way out, loosening the fan belt and causing the engine to overheat and the battery to discharge. The bolt was nowhere to be found.

"What are we going to do?" my friend asked I desperation. He didn't want a blemish on his service record, and I wasn't thrilled with the idea myself.

"You're the one who's religious," I said sarcastically. "Why don't you pray?"

As he walked away, I searched for a bolt or screw we would use as a replacement. No luck.

My friend came back looking remarkably calm. "I took your advice," he said. "Everything will be all right."

There was the rumbling of a huge tractor-trailer coming toward us. As it passed, I heard a clink on the road and felt something hit my foot. I looked down to see a bolt that must have fallen off the truck. I picked it up and twisted it in. It fit perfectly!

Thirty years have passed and I can still feel that little piece of steel hitting my foot. It really was a bolt out of the blue - or out of heaven.

No Food in the House

Adele Hooker

I have always had a strong faith in God, but I had never looked for miracles in my life. Until years ago . . .

When our family of four lived in Muskogee, Oklahoma, our income was so small that we could barely pay for necessities. Sometimes we ate cornflakes and milk for a week. On one such occasion, friends travelling through town stopped in; to my amazement, my husband invited them for dinner.

I fidgeted, then went into my bedroom, knelt down, and asked God how I was to cook a dinner with no food in the house.

"But you have," came the answer that formed in my head. "You have meat in the freezer." (I didn't believe it.) "You have vegetables." (Maybe a can of beans.) "Make a stew. And you have flour. Make biscuits." (That I could do. I'm a good biscuit builder.)

I went to the kitchen to prove my inner voice wrong, but there in the freezer lay a small amount of hamburger, in the crisper lay half an onion and a carrot; and in the bin under the sink were two small potatoes.

I made the stew. Hadn't I asked God for help? What could I do but follow the directions that seemed to come to me? I put the flimsy fare in a pot, mixed up the biscuits, and set the table.

When I poured the stew, there was just enough to fill a medium serving bowl. My husband and I would eat only biscuits and milk. But when I passed the stew around, behold, there was plenty. I served us and passed the bowl around again!

When our dinner was over, the guests thanked me for the delicious meal. And I gathered up leftovers.

We had leftovers. We did, we really did!

A Scrawny Mutt Named Buck

Joy Thames

I had coaxed him out from under my daddy's truck, a scrawny mutt I named Buck. We quickly became inseparable.

In September 1989, under threat of hurricane Hugo, my family evacuated our mobile home and went to my uncle's place on the Awendaw Creek. Sixteen of us filled the small house. For a while I stood on the front porch with Buck, watching the tall pines break in the wind.

Around midnight, the creek began rising rapidly, and we had to fight our way through the flooding house and upstairs. In the confusion I left Buck outside.

I tried to go back, but my mother stopped me. "The water's still rising!" she yelled. But what about Buck? He'd never survive the turbulent waters outside. I did the only thing I could think of: I begged God to shelter my friend.

After a few hours, the water dropped. We went downstairs. I sloshed through the three-in-thick mud to the front door. No Buck. I walked through the dank house to the screened-in back porch. The door was still tightly latched. I started to cry.

Just then I heard a whimper. Huddled on the porch swing was Buick! I rubbed my face in his soggy coat. "How did you . . ."

Something dripped on me, and I looked up to see a small rip in the screen near the ceiling, twenty feet from the ground. I looked at Buck and then back at the rip. It was the one opening to the house. The creek must have risen just high enough for Buck to wriggle inside - to shelter.

In the Midst of a Storm

Joan Shelton

On vacation in Mexico, my husband, Dick, and I rigged our Windsurfers on the beach and sailed into the Caribbean.

Dick was several hundred yards ahead of me when suddenly the wind picked up and flipped me into the ocean. By the time I swam back to my board, we were in the midst of a tropical storm.

I tried to pull the sail out of the water, but the wind and rain overpowered me. I couldn't find Dick anywhere. I clung to the board: I knew if I lost hold if it, I could drown.

At that moment, in the swirling rain, I saw an enormous cruise ship headed directly toward me. I would never be able to get out of its way! Paralyzed with feat, I thought of our two young children back home and closed my eyes in prayer, "Lords, save me."

When I opened my eyes, the ship was veering away.

As the sea calmed Dick sailed toward me. "Let's get to shore while we can," he said.

Nearing the beach I spotted a friend of ours waving his arms in a frenzy. Before I was out of the water he called out, "Did you see it?"

"What?" I asked.

"The waterspout. It went across the water, right toward you. Then, just like that," he snapped his fingers, "it disappeared."

Is that why the cruise ship turned? I'll never know. I only know that in my time of need, God answered my prayer.

The Key on the Canned Ham

Helen S. McCutcheon

It was 5.30pm when my three children and I left the grocery store; in order to be home before dark, we took a shortcut. A cold mist fell - the dreariness of a February dusk in Michigan.

When we came to the train tracks, my six-year-old, Lynda, tripped and fell, and her right foot became wedged between the wooden tie and the steel track.

"Untie you shoe, honey, and slip your foot out," I said. But Lynda had already pulled her shoelace into a tight knot. I tried to unravel the knot with my house key, and then with a hairpin. Still it held fast. I tried yanking Lynda's foot free of the shoe, but it wouldn't come. I had to get the knot untied.

Starting to worry, I scooted my other two children down the embankment, then dropped my bag of groceries and ran back to Lynda.

Just then I felt a faint vibration. An approaching train! I dug at the knot - ripping my nails and bloodying my fingers. Lynda and I both broke into fearful sobbing.

"Oh, my God" I cried, "Help us. Please, God."

Two little faces stared up at me from the ditch, terror-stricken. My eyes then strayed to the spilled bag of groceries.

"The ham!" I screamed in a strange fit of revelation. I grabbed the canned ham, ripped the key from its bottom and peeled off the lid. Using the sharp edge of the lid, I severed the shoelace and pulled Lynda out of her shoe. In the glare and roar of the oncoming train we tumbled into the ditch. We were safe.

I've heard it said that God gives us what we need when we need it. I've since wondered, what did the Lord give me just then? The sharp lid of a can or an imagination sharpened to the quick?

No Time to Look

Sally Waltman

That June day our dog, Peanut, scampered along behind me on my morning jog. Only months before I had sold my home and moved to this neighbourhood with my son, Michael.

Because big dogs weren't allowed in our apartment, we had been forced to give away our large Airedale terrier. We were heartbroken. Meanwhile eight-year-old Michael began having problems in school. "Get a new dog." The psychologist advised.

That was how the small brown mutt running at my heels was rescued from the pound. She had an immediate positive effect on Michael's behaviour. She was also a great running companion.

We were almost home when I looked behind me. Peanut was gone. She must have wandered off on the wooded lot nearby. I called and looked, to no avail.

At home Michael burst into tears when I told him the news, but there was no more time to look. I had to hurry to work, and he had to go to his first day of summer camp.

"Let's pray," I said. Michael trusted that God would help us find Peanut, and I prayed that Michael wouldn't be disappointed if Peanut didn't find her way home.

I dropped Michael off at camp, explaining the situation to the director. Minutes after I arrived at my job, Michael's camp counsellor was on the phone. I hadn't known she lived a block and a half away from us. Just before she left for work, she had found a little brown mutt in her yard and locked her in, intending to look for the owner later. It was Peanut.

God Showed Me

Derek Best

My bride, Kasey, and I were visiting her family in Albuquerque, New Mexico, for Thanksgiving when an ice storm hit. I worried about the long drive home on slippery mountain roads.

"I'll give you a set of tyre chains," my father-in-law said. "You know how to use them, don't you?"

"Sure. Thanks," I said. I'd never actually put chains on tyres before; but I didn't want to seem incompetent, or worse, have my father-in-law think I wasn't capable of taking care of his daughter.

I crouched beside the right rear wheel and unrolled one of the chains. It had two rows of heavy metal links that I laid out on the ground behind the tyre. Then I slowly drove the car in reverse until the chains were positioned underneath the wheel. But when I brought the ends together to fasten the clasp, they wouldn't meet.

My fingers grew numb from the bitter cold as I struggled to connect the chains. No matter what I did, they wouldn't reach far enough. There was a two-inch gap between the ends. Lord, how in the world does this work? Letting go the ends of the chains, I buried my head in my hands, utterly frustrated.

When I looked back at the tyre, I couldn't believe my eyes. The chains were hooked together around the tyre! I examined them more carefully. There was a small lever that could be pushed to extend the length of the chain. So that's the way you do it.

God showed me how to put chains on one of the tyres. Now I knew how to finish the job myself.

Miraculous Healing

Pray one for another, that he may be healed. The effectual fervent prayer of a righteous man availeth much.

James 5:16

An Unburdened Mind

David Snitker

After a welding-torch accident, I lay in intensive care with eighty percent of my body burned; but I felt the presence of God, and I knew I was not going to die. I felt protected by the prayers of my family and friends. I was buoyed by an ecumenical prayer chain, by the children's Sunday school class and their get-well cards, and by the high-school athletes who raised money for my hospital bills.

Then, as I began to improve, some discomforting thoughts entered my mind. "Why do I deserve all this love?" I asked myself. "I've made a lot of mistakes. I've done things I'm ashamed of."

Suddenly I slipped into a relapse. My temperature climbed and I stopped making progress. In my feelings of guilt, I had stopped calling on God. Then one night, to my surprise, I found myself asking a nurse to read to me from the Bible.

She picked up my Bible and began to read from it at random. "Out of the depths have I cried unto Thee, O Lord . . ."

It was Psalm 130 - the perfect prayer for a man who felt unworthy!

"If Thou, Lord, shoulders mark iniquities, O Lord, who shall stand? But there is forgiveness with Thee . . . with the Lord there is mercy . . ."

When she finished, she routinely took my temperature. But the look on her face when she read the thermometer was not at all routine. "It's down," she said. "You're better!"

What strange events! God had saved my life; then I'd let my guilt get in the way of His healing power. But He wouldn't have it! He used a nurse and a Scripture verse to unburden my mind so He could finish healing my body - completely.

A Matter of Trust

Joanna Daniel

The headaches and exhaustion that had plagued me for weeks were getting worse. Finally a specialist diagnosed my problem as hemolysis - the destruction of the red blood cells. The type I had was fatal, and usually in a matter of months. I was only forty-five, with a husband and three children to care for.

"Your blood cells are bursting like little balloons," doctors said. "But we don't know why. Your condition is so advanced that any treatments are just too risky. All we can do is wait."

Alone in a hospital room, I was nauseous with fear. I was especially concerned for my little daughter Marcia. She was my Down syndrome child; how would she get along?

Whenever Marcia was frightened, she'd call out, "Devil, take your hands off me! I'm God's property!" She'd heard that on television.

We'd always smiled at her simple trust. Yet now I wondered if I had enough faith to say those words - and mean them? With unusual boldness, I said, "Satan, take your hands off me! I'm God's child and I won't die till He's through with me!"

Almost immediately, the nausea left. I felt Christ's presence!

I went home, but returned to the hospital three times a week for blood tests. By the second visit, the doctor reported that my blood count had climbed three points. "What's happening?" he asked, bewildered.

Five months later - without drugs or treatment of any kind - my blood count was normal. There was no trace of the hemolysis. The doctors were astounded, but I wasn't.

Today I often take Marcia in my arms, hold her tightly, and say, "Devil, get away! We're both God's property!"

A Heartfelt Prayer

Ellen St. John Barnwell

"Speak to me, Lord, and speak through me." It was my daily prayer, and I said it that Sunday at St. Luke's. On the altar, red roses glowed - roses I had provided in memory of my mother. When the service was over, I turned to my son Bob. "After we have dinner, let's take the altar flowers to Miss Marie."

"Good idea," he agreed. Mother and Miss Marie, now in her eighties, had been close friends.

Driving home, humming the recessional hymn together, we broke off at the same moment. "Let's take the flowers to Miss Marie now." The identical thought had occurred to both of us.

"What made you change your mind?" I asked as Bob turned the car toward Miss Marie's house.

"I don't know," was all he could say.

"I don't either," I hesitated. "But let's not waste any time."

Miss Marie's daughter Alice answered the doorbell. "How nice!" she said as I handed her the roses. "I've been in bed with the flu." She gestured vaguely. "Mother was resting in her room. Let me see if she's awake now."

We heard a sharp cry.

Bob and I raced down the hall. Miss Marie lay unconscious on the floor. Bob lifted her to her bed, I dialled the ambulance, and

Alice began sponging Miss Marie's forehead with cool water. Her eyes fluttered.

"Lucky you got to her in time," the medic told us. "When it's a little stroke they can't call for help."

"Couldn't speak," Miss Marie murmured. "Prayed to God in my heart."

That made two prayers He'd answered loud and clear.

The Ruby Light

Eros M. Savage

One cold early evening many years ago, my wife, Bartie, and I set out in our cabin cruiser for a picnic dinner on south San Francisco Bay. We waved to a college crew team heading out for a practice row, then proceeded down the channel toward the San Mateo Bridge. The choppy water soon turned into huge waves.

At the drawbridge, I signalled to the bridge tender to let us through. He shook his head, pointing to the whitecaps on the water ahead. We were about to take our pitching craft home when, in the distance near some mud flats, we saw a ruby-coloured light glowing, shimmering in the shape of a cross. Bartie and I were mesmerized. We turned our craft in the light's direction.

It was irresponsible of me - in shallow muddy water an engine might suck up mud that can destroy it - but I felt compelled to follow the cross. Now mud was coming from the exhaust pipe, and the temperature of our engine had risen into the danger zone; but the light drew me on.

We came up to the light, only to find that it was merely a buoy reflecting the red sunset. Bartie and I felt foolish; we had actually risked our boat to chase a mirage.

"Look, the water is full of coconuts," Bartie said. But they weren't coconuts at all; they were the men from the rowing crew whose shell had crashed into the bridge and sunk. One by one we pulled them aboard. They had been in the water for over an hour. Facing death and gulping the icy salt water, they had come to a point of desperation and had prayed together for rescue.

And that was when the cross began to shine for me.

Praying for an Egg

Josephine M. Kuntz

At one point during the winter of 1940, my husband, a house painter, was temporarily unemployed due to the weather; and the textile plant where I worked was closed due to a seasonal lay-off. We literally had no money. To make matters worse, our eighteen-month-old daughter, Rachel, was recovering poorly from pneumonia; and the doctor insisted we feed her a boiled egg each day. Even that was beyond our means.

"Why not pray for an egg?" suggested our baby sitter, who was staying on without pay to help us. We were a churchgoing family, but this teenager's depth of faith was something new to us at the time. All the same, she and I got on our knees and told the Lord that Rachel needed an egg each morning. We left the problem in His hands.

About ten o'clock that morning, we heard some cackling coming from the hedge fence in front of our house. There among the bare branches sat a fat red hen. We had no idea where she had come from. We just watched in amazement as she laid an egg and then proceeded down the road, out of sight.

The little red hen that first day was a surprise, and we thanked God for it; but can you imagine how startled we were when we heard the hen cackling in the hedge the next morning? And the morning after that, and the morning after that? Every day for over a week, Rachel had a fresh boiled egg.

Rachel grew better and better, and at last the weather turned and my husband went back to work. The next morning I waited by the window and watched. But our prayers had been answered - precisely.

The little red hen did not come back. Ever.

Please Keep me Safe

Kristina Seidel

The coach complemented me on the great practice I was having at the gym. I went from one event to the next, running through the gymnastics routines I wanted to master for competition.

When I got to the uneven bars, I was tired and sweaty; but I was still determined to attempt the dismount I'd been practicing in the pit, a rectangle filled with foam that provided a soft landing. This time I was psyched to try it on the mats.

"Dear God," I prayed as I climbed up o the bar, "please keep me safe. Amen."

Hanging by my hands, body extended, I swung once around the bar. I placed my feet outside my chalked hands and snapped into the air, flipping forward . . .

I'd released too early. I didn't have the height to complete a flip and land on my feet. Suddenly, in mid-arc, I felt my coach push me so that the upper part of my body landed safely on the mat. The rest of me crashed down on the thin layer of carpet that covered the cement floor.

While Coach iced my back, I remembered my prayer. Why hadn't God helped me as I'd asked, I wondered.

The pain was excruciating. My fall would probably keep me out of gymnastics for a while, but I realised that I could have been paralyzed if my head and neck hadn't landed on the mat. I thanked my coach for the push that saved me.

He looked at me, puzzled. "Krissy," he said, "you flew off that bar so fast, no one had time to get anywhere near you."

Locked in to Think

Doug Jennings

After seven years of marriage, I had filed for divorce and considered myself a single man. That's why I was surprised when my wife, Laura Lee, drove from our home in Florida to upstate New York to see me play for the Rochester Red Wings, a Baltimore Orioles farm team.

"What are you doing here?" I asked. "We're through."

That night I was unable to get Laura Lee out of my mind. I thought about how happy we had been before our troubles.

"Am I doing the right thing, Lord?" I asked.

On a road trip, a team mate introduced me to a friend and I asked her out for coffee. After getting ready in my motel room, I walked to the door. When I turned the knob it simply spun in my hand.

I flopped onto the bed and called the front desk. While waiting for help, I turned on the radio and heard a familiar song - the song Laura Lee and I danced to at our wedding! I remembered how I had held Laura Lee as we danced. Oh, how I missed her.

A custodian finally jimmied the door. I met my date, but my heart was still back in that locked room so I cut the date short.

When our team returned to Rochester, Laura Lee was waiting

for me. We started talking and in a couple of days we reconciled. I moved back home where I belonged.

I knew it was meant to be, because when the custodian got that motel room door open, he had said, "I don't see any reason why it wouldn't open."

Maybe he didn't, but I did.

Vision Restored

Don Bell

In the last few years, my vision has deteriorated. The only way I get around is by looking out of the corner of my eye. Most days I resemble a lame rooster with his head half-cocked, tripping over furniture in my own house.

Then came an April night not long ago when a loud knock on the door roused me from sleep. A young man said there was a fire behind my property. In my rush, I bumped into a table and knocked over a lamp. My wife, Vera, came to see what the racket was. Our neighbour's tool shed was ablaze! "I'll call the fire department," said Vera, and I raced outside.

I banged on the Jensens' door to wake them up. The tool shed was attached to their garage. We didn't have much time; the garage's fibreglass siding was melting from the encroaching flames. "Lord," I said "my neighbour needs me. Be my strength."

We shoved the garage doors open and moved the car and pick-up truck to safety. Next we hauled out lawn mowers and tools, everything we could get our hands on. I surveyed the contents and tried to rescue the most valuable equipment first. Finally we heard sirens.

After the firefighters had confined the blaze, my neighbour

thanked me. "You saw clearly what had to be done, Don," he said.

Back home I tripped over a chair, straining to see the hot cup of coffee Vera put in front of me. "You saw clearly . . ." the neighbour had said. And I had. When I needed it most, the Lord had restored my vision.

A Runaway Bus

Evelyn McKay

Elmer Hambaugh will never forget that Easter weekend shortly after he became a Christian - especially that Monday morning when the doctors came to operate on his foot.

Good Friday morning, thinking to take a short work break, Elmer parked the city bus he drove for a living in front of a suburban Cincinnati police station. As he chatted inside, Elmer was dumbstruck to see his empty bus start slowly to roll downhill, straight for an intersection packed with rush-hour traffic.

He raced out, praying, "Dear God, stop that bus!"

In an absurdly heroic effort, Elmer grabbed hold of the side-panel advertisement on the vehicle and dug in his heels - only to be knocked down and dragged under the chassis, one foot caught wedge-like between a rolling rear wheel and the pavement.

Then, for no apparent reason, the bus came to a halt.

There it stood, neatly parked at a crosswalk, safely behind the white line. A city maintenance worker - a man who'd never driven a bus - rushed to Elmer's rescue and managed to back up the vehicle.

Doctors at the hospital shook their heads when they saw Elmer's lacerated flesh and mangled foot. Anticipating a complicated skin graft, they scheduled a Monday morning operation.

All weekend Elmer prayed and fasted, stoic about his own pain as he concentrated on Christ's greater torment. And on Easter Monday, he heard the doctors' words of amazement - words that told of something even stranger than the fact that the bus had suddenly stopped. "Your foot has healed," they said. "There's no reason to operate."

Mysterious Strangers

Hear my prayer, O Lord . . .
for I am a stranger with thee,
and a sojourner, as all my fathers were.

Psalm 39:12

Then he Vanished

Euphie Eallonardo

It had been reckless of me, taking a predawn stroll through the tangle of streets behind the Los Angeles bus terminal. But I was a young woman arriving in the great city for the first time. My job interview was five hours away, and I couldn't wait to explore!

Now I'd lost my way in a skid row neighbourhood. Hearing a car pass, I turned and, in the flash of light, saw three men lurking behind me, trying to keep out of sight in the shadows. Trembling with fright, I did what I always do when in need of help. I bowed my head and asked God to rescue me.

When I looked up, a fourth man was striding toward me in the dark! Dear God, I thought, I'm surrounded. I was so scared that it took me a few seconds to realise that even in the blackness, I could see this man. He was dressed in an immaculate work shirt and denim pants, and he carried a lunchbox. He was about thirty and well over six feet tall. His face was stern but beautiful.

I ran up to the man. "I'm lost and some men are following me" I said in desperation. "I took a walk from the bus depot - I'm so scared."

"Come," he said, "I'll take you to safety."

He was strong and made me feel safe.

"I . . . I don't know what would have happened if you hadn't come along," I said.

"I do." His vice was resonant, deep.

"I prayed for help just before you came."

A smile touched his mouth and eyes. We were nearing the depot. "You are safe now."

"Thank you so much," I said fervently.

He nodded. "Good-bye, Euphie."

Going into the lobby, it hit me. Euphie! Had he really used my first name? I whirled and burst out onto the sidewalk. But he had vanished.

No Footprints Left Behind

M. M. McIntosh

A misty rain fell on our construction crew as we climbed a mountain near La Grande, Oregon. Our job was to remove rock from a pipeline ditch and put in a gas line.

As the swamper, I cleaned mud from the heavy machinery parts and then greased them. I was still working when the other guys decided to break for lunch and take off to a point about one thousand feet down the mountain. "Meet us when you can, Mac," they called out.

By the time I finished, I was soaking wet, and muddy and greasy from head to foot. There was no way I could eat my lunch without washing first. I looked into the ditch, which was filled with water. Easy way to wash up, I thought. I jumped in, expecting to stand knee-deep in water, but instead I was completely immersed. And to make matters worse, my boots were stuck in mud up to my shins.

Frantically I tugged at one leg and then the other, only to be pulled in deeper. Mud had reached my chest and the weight of the water was pressing down. "Oh, God," I prayed, "please help."

Finally I could hold my breath no longer. I exhaled and felt my body descend. My throat burned as the muddy water rushed inside me. Then I blacked out.

The next thing I knew I was lying face down on the bank of the ditch, as if I had been dragged to safety. I looked for one of the crew. No one was there. No muddy footprints, no tracks, no evidence of help . . . except His.

A Black Labrador on the Porch

Rev. John E. Troncale

My very first assignment as a minister was to an inner city parish in Camden, New Jersey. Drug dealing and violent crime took place within sight of our home, and rough characters knocked on our door at all hours of the day and night.

Not long after we arrived, I had to attend a week-long church conference out of town. I dreaded leaving my wife and three children along in our new neighbourhood. "God," I prayed, "take care of them."

My first spare moment at the conference, I called home to make sure all was well. My wife assured me that everything was fine and that no one had bothered them. "But there is one thing, she said. "You barely gotten out the door when a huge black Labrador retriever ambled up to our front porch and lay down. Now he won't leave."

"Don't feed him or touch him," I said. "He's probably one of our neighbour's. He'll go back where he belongs soon enough."

The next day when I called, the dog still hadn't left the front porch. "He never bothers the children or me, but he won't let anyone else come to the door," my wife said. "Not even the mailman!"

At the end of the conference, I returned home to find the big black dog sitting on our front porch. He stood up when I opened the car door, his eyes trained on my every move.

Once I reached the steps, I said tentatively, "Hey boy, I've got to get in the house to be with my family," With that, he stepped aside.

After hugging my wife and kids, I asked her what we should do about the dog. "I don't know," she said. "I have to admit, I felt completely safe knowing he was out there keeping watch."

We both looked to the porch. The dog was gone. I went outside and walked around the block, checking all the front porches. No sign of the big retriever! It was as if he had vanished off the face of the earth.

And perhaps he had.

Footprints to Follow

Sandy Seltzer

Dustin, my California-bred guide dog, was having trouble outside our Long Island apartment. This was his first snowstorm and he was confused. I'm blind, and I wasn't doing so well either. No one was out, so there were no sounds to steer me. And contrary to what many people think, guide dogs do not find the way for a blind person. The blind person directs the dog.

After a harrowing forty-five minutes, Dustin and I finally made it back. But guide dogs must be walked regularly. "Next time why don't you ask God to go with you?" a friend suggested. And so I did. "Lord, go with Dustin and me. The wind is so fierce, it's hard to concentrate on our direction. Lead us."

Snow stung our faces and it was difficult to make a path. Dustin whined a little. "Okay, boy," I said to him, "the Lord is with us." And then I gave him a command that a blind person gives only when another person is leading the way: "Dustin, follow!"

Dustin perked up and to my astonishment took off as though he knew exactly where to go. We made it to the street and then headed back to our building with no problem.

A young woman trudged up and offered to walk us to our door. "We'll just follow your footprints," she said, "Yours and the dog's, and that other person's.

"What other person?" I asked.

"There are a dog's prints. And your prints. And a larger person's prints. Wasn't someone with you?"

I paused for a moment and then I answered, "Oh yes, there was Someone with us." There always is.

Swallowed by the Fog

Mary Pettit Holmes

I had to stay late that evening at the bloodmobile, where I am a registered nurse working with the American Red Cross. By the time I trudged out to my car, it was dark and fog was rolling in. I had an hour's drive home to our small town that is nestled near the base of the coastal range.

The traffic was light, which was good, because the fog was getting heavier. I could barely see the white line at the edge of the freeway and the street lamps that lit it. Then I turned off onto our country road. Ten more miles to drive on a narrow, twisting road with deep ditches and a stream alongside.

"Help me, Lord," I prayed. Recently in church we had been discussing the use of mental imaging while praying. Now I visualised Jesus sitting next to me in the passenger seat. I poured out my fears to Him.

Hugging the steering wheel I stared at the eerie whiteness. Suddenly, ahead of me I saw the red taillights of another car. Slowly I drew closer. The red taillights were on an orange pickup being hauled by a tow truck. I was relieved. Undoubtedly the pickup was being taken to the garage in Forest Grove. If I followed it, I could make it home.

We came to Main Street - but we passed the repair shop. The tow truck drove on. It kept going. Then to my amazement, it turned onto the dead-end road where we lived. With a sigh of relief I turned into our driveway, then I quickly got out to thank the driver of the tow truck that had led me home.

There was no driver. There was no tow truck. It had not turned around to exit from the dead end. I stood staring into the silent fog at the end of our road.

An All-Powerful Light

Muriel S. Hurst

My daughter Sandi and I were driving home to Tennessee after spending Thanksgiving with relatives in Detroit. As we neared the Cumberland Mountains, we hit a blinding snowstorm. The radio warned of treacherous conditions. Phone lines were down. Ours was the lone car approaching the foothills.

Straightening in her seat, Sandi gripped the steering wheel tightly. "Let's keep going. Dad's expecting us," she said.

I was anxious to get back home too. "Okay," I agreed. "let's keep going."

We started uphill. I strained to see the signs marking the winding road, but the wipers were no match for the driving snow. "I can't see," Sandi said.

I had made a terrible decision. We couldn't turn around. "God, please guide us," we prayed aloud.

"Look!" I shouted. A glowing light shone hazily in the distance, about fifty feel ahead. "Follow that vehicle!" Snow covered the road signs, but the light moved on steadily, like a beacon.

An hour passed, and we began our descent. The light slowed, and through every bend and dip in the road, the distance between us remained constant until finally we rounded the last curve. We looked ahead. Not one other vehicle was on the road.

We wanted to thank our guide. "He's got to be in here," Sandi said, pulling into a diner. When we walked I, the customers stared.

"How did you get over that mountain?" the waitress asked. "No one has come across in hours."

The all-powerful Light had guided us.

My Driving Companion

Dorothy Howard

I was driving home after visiting my family for Christmas. Traffic on the two-land road was slow but steady. A fine mist saturated the cold air; and as the temperature dropped, the highway grew slick.

Suddenly my wheels skidded and the brakes locked. The guardrail was coming up fast! I cried out, "God, help me!"

The impact of the crash threw me over the seat and I blacked out. I woke up on the floor in the back seat. A man and his son were bent over me.

"You hit a patch of ice," the man said. "A policeman saw the whole thing. He's calling for help."

Peering out the window, I realised that my car had been moved to the opposite side of the highway and parked safely on the grass off the shoulder. How in the world did I get over here? I wondered. Before I could ask, another car hit the same patch of ice and spun into the guardrail - at the exact spot I had. The man and his son ran to help.

When trucks arrived to sand the road, father and son returned with the policeman. "By the way," the policeman said, "what happened to your companion?"

"The man who drove the car to this spot," the officer said. "I saw him."

"We saw him too," said the father. "He crossed the lane of oncoming traffic and parked right here. But no one got out. In fact, we had to break a window to get in."

There had been no man in my car. But Someone had been with me.

The Kindness of Strangers

Cheryl Toth

Our car broke down in the middle of the western Texas desert, fifty miles from the nearest town. My kids and I tried to flag down some help, but no one stopped. Finally I sat down behind the wheel and prayed to the Lord to help us.

In time, a small blue Toyota truck pulled up and an older couple stepped out. To my amazement, the woman said, "We were on another highway and we heard in our prayers that someone needed our help."

The man said he was a mechanic. He looked under the hood of my car and told me that because of a malfunctioning alternator, my battery was dead.

"We'll take the battery to get it recharged," he said. They left us some sandwiches to eat and a red toolbox full of valuable tools to assure me of their return.

After two hours they came back with a new battery, which the man installed. Then his wife placed her hands gently on my cheeks and said, "You'll be all right, Cheryl."

She turned to my young children and added, "Michael and Janet, be good to your mommy. See that she gets home safely to Indiana."

They got in their truck. Only after they had driven away did it occur to me: They knew my name. They knew my children's names. They knew where we were going. But we had told them none of these things.

The Ever-Present Comforter

And I will pray the Father,
and he shall give you another Comforter,
that he may abide with you for ever.

John 14:16

A Name with Meaning

RHONDA VECERA NAYLOR

My paternal grandmother, who immigrated to this country from Czechoslovakia, died when I was eighteen. I missed her, especially at the big events in my life, such as my marriage and the birth of my first child.

I often caught myself thinking back to Nanny's cosy kitchen, where she let me help her roll out dough for pastries and strudels while regaling me with tales of her old-world girlhood. Though her jumbled English translations of Czech phrases were often stumbling blocks, I always knew that Nanny loved me.

When we had our second daughter, my husband, Ronny, decided he didn't like the name we had agreed on months earlier. I was taken aback by his abrupt change. On the day I was to come home from the hospital, we still hadn't picked a name! I wished Nanny were here.

"God," I finally prayed, "help us get over this stumbling block and find the perfect name."

We named the baby Kinsey, a name Ronny liked. I had a hard time getting used to it and often wondered during that first year if I ever would. Then one day we got a letter from my mom, containing the death certificate of my dad's brother. Mom had drawn an arrow pointing to the space where my grandmother's maiden name was listed. I had only known her Czech last name: Komina. Now I gazed in wonderment at the English version: Kinsey.

Every day now when I look into Kinsey's cheery face, I see a godly reminder of my grandmother's lasting love.

Words of Comfort

Nancy Bayless

The first day my husband, Lynn, received chemotherapy for bone marrow cancer, I was overwhelmed with sadness. We live on a boat, and that night I worried about him and all the work that was now my responsibility.

At midnight, as I was preparing for bed, I ran out of paper towels. In the darkness of the main cabin, I found a new double-roll package in a locker. I ripped open the cellophane and took out a roll.

I always buy plain white to go with our red, white and blue décor. In the light I could see this roll was covered with pink flowers - it was all wrong!

Somehow that did it. I burst into tears, "Lord, I can't even buy the right paper towels!" I wailed to God, wallowing in self-pity. How, I wondered, will I varnish the boat? How will I maintain the engine? How will I go on without Lynn?

Finally, my tears were spent. I picked up the roll of paper towels, and as I put it in the holder, I noticed there was writing among the pink flowers. One sheet read "Friendship is a special gift." Those words made me think of all the friends I could call on at any hour.

The next words were "Love is sharing." I thought of the gifts we had been given - casseroles, cookies, hugs. Then "No act of love, however small, is ever wasted" reminded me of the telephone calls and other kindnesses we had received. I felt at peace.

The next morning I opened the locker again. Inside the town cellophane was the second roll of paper towels. It was not covered with flowers - it was plain white.

When Hearts Appear

Sue Monk Kidd

Hearts. My mother always had a special feeling about hearts. When I had chicken pox as a child, I remember her cheering me with heart-shaped peanut butter sandwiches. For years she embroidered heart designs on Raggedy Ann dolls to give away. Hearts were her gift of love, especially in difficult times.

And so, when my niece Laura was born with a serious physical defect and was fighting for her life, I wasn't surprised to find Mama in the waiting room, quietly sewing a tiny valentine heart onto a rag doll. I knew Mama was suffering. I even remembered her saying once that she couldn't bear the thought of a grand-child dying.

I prayed that day for little Laura, but I also prayed, "Please, Lord, be with Mama too."

Weeks passed with no improvement in Laura's health, nor in Mama's spirits. At last, my parents decided to visit their country farm. I pictured the little grey farmhouse nestled under the big, spreading pecan tree; and I hoped that there Mama might find peace.

A day later my phone rang. It was Mama. She asked me if I remembered how in June the pecan tree always shed its stringy seed tassels. I said I did.

Mama then said, "You know how badly I've needed to feel God's closeness. Well, Daddy and I were about to sweep the tassels off the porch when we looked down, and there I noticed one tassel in particular. Just guess how it was shaped."

Before I could guess, Mama joyously exclaimed, "It was in the perfect shape of a heart!"

A Tiny Bud Vase

Charlotte Doty

November 3 was my birthday. As I drove down the mountainside to Holy Apostles Episcopal Church in Hilo that Sunday morning, I couldn't help but miss Mother.

It had been six months since her death, and this would be the first birthday I had to celebrate without her - without the cake she always baked and the table she always decorated with yellow roses.

Our family had lived in Hawaii for fifty years, but Texas-born Mother was always "The Yellow Rose of Texas," and her house filled with that mainland flower.

At church I slipped into the pew. "I miss Mother so," I sort of prayed, kneeling with my head in my hands. I couldn't bring myself to look at the flower-filled urns on their tall koa-wood stands. The brilliant orchids and anthuriums could only clash with my grey mood inside.

The first hymn brought me unwillingly to my feet. And that was when I saw it, not on the stands where flowers were always placed, but right on the altar: a tiny bud vase. And in the vase was a single yellow rose.

This was the best birthday gift I would have received, this reminder that those we love are never far away.

At the service's close, I hurried to the Flower Guild chairman to find out who had left this bud on the altar, a place I had never seen flowers before. She was as puzzled as I and told me that the vase didn't even belong to the church. And though we queried every guild member, and anyone else who might have brought flowers, no one could explain how the rose came to be there. To this day I don't know how - only Who.

A Comforting Rain

Sara Snipes

For Robert and me, rain was always heaven-sent. During our courtship there was not much money for entertainment; however, we always enjoyed walking together - particularly in the rain. And the rain poured continually on our wedding day.

For the next twenty-one years of our marriage, Robert often told of stopping for gas in my little town of Watkinsville on the way to our wedding. Since Robert was from south Georgia, no one knew him. The owner of the gas station laughed and told Robert about some poor nut who was getting married in this downpour. Some poor nut indeed!

For our wedding, Robert had had an inscription engraved inside my ring, but I didn't know what it read until I removed the ring as he checked us into our honeymoon suite. There I saw the words, Because You Walked with Me in the Rain.

Through the years of child-rearing, the loss of parents, the moves and the worries about jobs - no matter what the problem - our faith in God remained steadfast. We always took comfort in His Word, just like it says in Deuteronomy, "My words shall fall upon you like the gentle rain." (The Living Bible)

Then one night Robert died suddenly from a heart attack. Soon family and friends gathered around me; but, after they left, I didn't want to go to bed. I felt so alone. I wandered outside and stood on the front porch. The night was quiet; the sky was clear. And then, for only a few remarkable seconds, there came the familiar, comforting, reassuring sound of raindrops - splattering on the sidewalk before me.

His Name was Bakht Singh

Edward A. Elliott

It meant a day out of our vacation, but my wife and I strongly felt that we should make the effort while we were in Maine to go see Dr. Reuben Larson, an eighty-year-old missionary pioneer.

After lunch during our visit, quite out of the blue, Dr. Larson asked, "Ed, in all your travels, have you ever run into an Indian named Bakht Singh?"

How extraordinary! Only two weeks before, on one of his infrequent visits to the United States, Bakht Singh had invited me to lunch.

I told Dr. Larson what I'd learned about Singh - how he was one of India's best-known Christian leaders and how he had founded hundreds of churches and had preached to thousands. Whenever Singh travelled, believers gathered at train stations to speak and pray with him for just a few minutes.

The things I told about this godly man had a strange effect on Dr. Larson. He was literally open-mouthed. Finally he explained why.

"Many years ago in western Canada, I met a young Indian engineering student who was interested in the Christian faith. His name was Bakht Singh. For fifty years I've been praying for him, praying that he would come to know God better and serve Him. I've always wondered what became of him."

It wasn't long after our visit that Dr. Larson died. But even before then I knew why we'd taken that day out of our vacation to see him. We were meant to bring him the news that he had waited fifty years to hear.

A Concert to Heal

Eugenia Eason

On July 4, 1945, I walked gloomily through the halls of a Chicago YWCA. I had come to the city for a crucial ear operation. The next day I would begin four days of preparation before surgery at Saint Luke's Hospital.

As a piano teacher, I was especially frightened about the outcome - the operation was so new that few others had had it. With no friends close by, I was lonely. I was apprehensive. "If only You would send me someone I could talk to," I prayed to God.

As I passed the solarium, I noticed a piano, almost as if it were the friend I needed. I felt drawn to the keyboard. I sat down at the piano and began to play. I played and played. The music flowered with a spirit of its own, expressing my pent-up feelings. At last I finished and got up to leave.

"Please, don't stop!" a voice called out. All this time, though I hadn't noticed her, a woman had been sitting in the far corner of the room.

We introduced ourselves and started to chat. She, too, was a stranger in town. And she, too, it turned out, had been through the very same surgery I was about to undergo, with "my" doctor at "my" hospital, exactly a year before! It was she who reassured me about the operation that in a few days would prove to be such a success.

She had heard my music. But Someone else had heard my prayer.

Found in the Right Place

Paul Heller

When I graduated from seminary, I acquired a handsome three-foot-long, purple, red, gold and black academic hood signifying the degree I'd earned. As a Presbyterian minister, I wore it over my black robe for special ceremonies, ordinations, and installations.

One day I opened my closet and it was not there. I couldn't remember when I'd last worn it or where I'd left it, but I quickly prayed that it was not lost.

At the time, I was pastor of a small congregation in the western hills of New York's huge Adirondack Forest Preserve. Then I was extended a call to serve as minister of a larger congregation in a more urban area on the shores of Lake Champlain. After considerable soul-searching, I accepted the call; but I prayed for reassurance that my decision was the right one.

I was greeted warmly by the staff and congregation at the new church. I had fond memories of a visit I had made there eight years earlier for an installation ceremony, but it was only when I opened the closet door in my new office that I knew I had done the right thing in coming to this church, this time to stay.

There I discovered my hood, waiting for me as it had waited patiently for eight years.

Not a Deer in Sight

Bob Rawlins

It was a cold winter night as my wife, my daughter, and I headed home from shopping. I was deep in thought because I had just accepted a job as the director of a boys' home. Now my decision was troubling me. Did I make the right choice in taking the position?

I drove carefully because it was not unusual to come across deer on the highway in this part of Indiana. That was it. "Lord," I said aloud, "if you love me, let me see a deer tonight."

"Oh, you know the Lord loves you," my wife said.

"Yes," I replied, "but I need reassurance that I am following His will."

My senses and vision were heightened as I drove. But nothing, not even an old farm cat, appeared. Disheartened, I turned into our gravel driveway and pulled into the garage. Nothing. Not a deer in sight.

While Jackie and Susannah juggled packages into the house, I trudged over to the mailbox. I pulled out a handful of letters and made my way to the front door while idly flipping through the mail. A bill, another bill, a fundraising letter, two Christmas cards, and then a third. I stopped. On the third card, glowing under the porch light, was a stamp; and on the stamp was unmistakably a deer.

In that moment, I knew I had made the right decision. I had seen God's deer. I had felt God's love.

The Name on the Pew

Irma Levesque

I grew up in rural New Hampshire, eldest daughter in a family of six children. In our chaotic household I found refuge in make believe, often pretending that I was a beautiful girl named "Joan Bishop" (Joan from Joan of Arc and Bishop from the English translation of my French last name). I never told anyone else about Joan Bishop. It was a secret between God and me.

Little girls grow up, though, and the day came when I bade goodbye to Joan Bishop . . . and to God. I moved to New York, got caught up in a fiercely competitive line of work, and gradually found my personal life getting lonelier and lonelier. In time I knew I wanted to return to God, but I hesitated. Would He welcome me back?

One Sunday morning I could not stay away any longer. I went to nearby Grace Church. I walked down the north aisle, pat the old pews, each with its own waist-high door and tiny brass nameplates - relics from the last century when parishioners purchased their seats. I chose an empty pew and closed the door behind me.

"Please, God," I began to pray, "I'm lonely and afraid. Are You here? Is this the place for me? Will these people all around me take me in?" I wanted God's assurance that I should stay in that church, but no assurance seemed to come. Suddenly I felt an overpowering urge to leave.

Hastily gathering up my coat and scarf, I opened the pew door and stepped into the aisle. As I turned to shut the old door, my eyes were drawn to its tiny brass nameplate. The plate read: J. Bishop.

I returned to my seat. I was home again.

A Lesson I'll Carry Always

Tim Rich

While a senior premed student at the University of Minnesota in Duluth, I lived down the street from a nursing home. Under a physician's guidance, I was responsible for several patients there. Late one evening I took a walk to stretch my legs. As I passed the nursing home, I thought of Zita.

She was one of my most difficult cases. She lay in a semi-comatose state, never uttering a word and never moving. Whenever I visited her, I held her hand and talked to her, but she had never reacted. In school we termed that "unresponsive." God, I wondered, am I doing any good?

But that night something came over me, and I knew I had to check on Zita. I let myself in through the front door and walked down the hall to her room.

As I glanced at her chart, I wondered why I had come. Suddenly a voice said, "Tim, I'm glad you came." It was Zita!

She pushed herself up on one elbow. "I wanted to thank you. You've been a wonderful doctor."

I patted her hand. "I'll be right back," I promised, and I rushed to get a nurse.

"Zita's responsive!" I said.

The nurse looked at me incredulously, and we dashed to Zita's room. She had resumed her usual position, eyes closed. I felt the side of her neck. There was a faint pulse, then she was gone.

But she had taught me a lesson I'll carry with me throughout my medical career: compassion is powerful medicine.

My Wake-Up Call

Marilyn Teets

"This has got to be the worst day of my life," I moaned. I was the administrator of a large retirement community in Spokane, and every hour at work seemed to bring another crisis. I needed to resolve my staff's salary and scheduling differences. A new sewer was being installed. I had just been told I might need back surgery. On top of it all, my daughter Teresa had just married and moved away. I missed her terribly.

"Nothing's going right. I can't handle it," I told God flatly as I got into my car and headed to a dinner meeting. On the freeway I saw police cars and heard sirens. What now? There had been an accident and I was trapped in gridlock. I'd be late for the meeting.

I pulled out my new cellular phone to call my mother. Maybe she could look up the restaurant's number and leave word that I would be late. But it wasn't Mom who answered; it was Teresa!

"Mom, I'm so glad you called," she said. "Yours is the first call we got since our phone was installed."

"But, Teresa, I didn't call you," I said. "I don't even know your new number."

"Really? I'm glad you're on the line anyway," she went on excitedly. "You're going to be a grandmother!"

Suddenly it was clear to me how blessed I was. With God's help I could handle whatever came my way: I just needed a wake-up call to jolt me out of my self-pity - and He had dialled the number.

Sustained by Words

Margaret Murray

In September 1983, Uncle Wilson, my mother's only brother, underwent surgery for an intestinal tumour. The doctors, discovering a tumour too large and complex to remove, gave him four to six months to live. Uncle Wilson was brought home for his remaining days. With no wife to see to his needs, his care fell to my mother, her two sisters, and us nieces and nephews.

We all worked hard to make Uncle Wilson comfortable, but he was bedridden, helpless, and in great pain. Day after day we tended to his needs and tried to soothe his fears. And every night before bed, I knelt and asked God to heal this good, kind man.

In July 1984, after ten hard months, Uncle Wilson took a turn for the worse. I was called and told to come at once. I stood by his bed, waiting for the ambulance to come. Even in his pain Uncle Wilson tried to communicate his love and thanks by kissing my hand.

By now I was no longer praying for his healing, but simply asking that God take my uncle to be with Him. And then, early in the morning of his third day in the hospital, my sister and I were with him when Uncle Wilson suddenly opened his eyes and in a loud and clear voice cried, "My God! My God! My God!" My sister and I were wonder-struck.

Uncle Wilson died soon after, but my family was sustained by his words. My uncle, you see, had been deaf and mute since birth. These words were the first he had even spoken.

Heavenly Music

Marian Thomson Scheirman

When I visited my parents at a retirement centre an hour's drive away, Mother always had me play the piano. We would go downstairs to the chapel, and I would give a private "concert" on the baby grand piano. For my father, I played hymns. For Mother, I played classical pieces, always including her favourite, Beethoven's "Für Elise."

After her ninetieth birthday, Mother lost her vitality. Late one afternoon when I visited, Mother rested on her bed, wearing her green paisley dress. "You'll play 'Für Elise' for me, won't you?" she asked. But she wasn't strong enough to go downstairs, and the nearby activity room that had an upright piano was locked.

"I'll come tomorrow and play for you," I promised. I left soon after. That night Mother died in her sleep.

The evening after her funeral, I wandered into my living room, where I sat down at the piano and played "Für Elise." Dear Lord, I thought, I didn't get to play it for Mother. It broke my heart to think that Mother would never hear her favourite music again.

Just then my phone rang. At first, the line was silent. Then came a series of musical notes - high, quick, and mechanical-sounding - but not like a music box or the sounds of a touch-toe phone.

Then I realised what those notes were. Through the phone receiver had come the first few phrases of Beethoven's "Für Elise." And I knew God was reminding me that where Mother was, the music was heavenly.

A Love of Daisies

Haven Conner

I never see a daisy without thinking of Barbara. We were sorority sisters in college. After her engagement, we searched for a silverware pattern - with daisies. As her bridesmaid I carried the same yellow and white flowers up the aisle, and daisies were everywhere at the reception.

Barbara and I talked every day, but then a terrible thing happened. I let an argument between our husbands drive a wedge between us. We stopped talking regularly and quit celebrating birthdays together. Suddenly we weren't friends anymore. I kept putting off calls to her to make things right, but the regret never left me. Then I learned that Barbara had died, at age thirty-eight.

I agonised over what had been left unsaid. One afternoon I slumped in a chair in my backyard, where we had held Barbara's wedding reception. "Oh, God," I prayed, "I'll never forgive myself for not telling Barbara how sorry I am and how much I loved her."

"Tell her now," God seemed to say.

I poured my heart out, just like we used to. "You were the best friend I ever had," I said. "I'm so sorry."

Somehow I felt Barbara had heard me. I got up, trimmed some wayward branches, and even mowed the grass. That night I went to bed with a lighter heart. I only wished that I had reached out to Barbara when she could still respond.

The next morning, in a corner of the yard, sprouting up from the freshly mowed lawn was an unexpected bouquet - a foot-high clump of yellow and white daisies.

His Last Words

Faye Field

On December 9, 1991, I had an unusual dream. I stood alone in a small auditorium. From backstage came a familiar voice: a young man reciting something I couldn't quite make out. Then he said, clearly, "Yea, though I walk through the valley of the shadow of death ..." I recognised it immediately as the Twenty-third Psalm! "I will fear no evil: for thou art with me . . ."

Suddenly the voice stopped and I woke up. It was 2:00am.

I realised the voice I my dream was that of a former student, my sister's son, Samuel C. Washam. The auditorium was in the rural school where I had taught him. He had a good voice and had often stepped out from behind the stage curtains in plays I directed. I had taught him many recitations, but the Twenty-third Psalm was one of his favourites.

Since then, I had prayed many times for my nephew, who was now middle-aged, terminally ill, and lonely. He was afraid and seemed to have lost his way from God. I had asked the Lord to let Samuel C. know that broken people are dear to his heart. I fell back into a fitful sleep with that same prayer on my lips.

The phone woke me early. It was my sister telling me her son had died. I asked her, "When?"

"Two o'clock this morning," she answered quietly.

I thought of the last words Samuel C. had said in my dream, "For thou art with me." I knew he had found his way again.

An Unmistakable Urge

Marion Bond West

When I married Gene after both our spouses had died, what I wanted most was to be a good minister's wife. His first wife, Phyllis, had been perfect at the task.

For twenty-five years she had been a church organist, organised women's groups, taught Bible classes, sang, counselled, planned church socials, and cooked marvellous meals. She was always patient, loving, supportive, and loyal. She even invited the entire congregation to their home for fellowship.

My biggest challenge came when Gene took an interim pastorate in Perry, Oklahoma. As we drove there, I struggled with unspoken feelings of deep inadequacy.

That summer morning, we were leaving a motel in Jackson, Tennessee, after visiting family in Georgia. Gene was preoccupied with loading the car and planning our day's drive. I picked up the Gideons Bible as I waited for him and prayed for guidance.

"Let's go," Gene finally announced, bags in hand. I started to replace the Bible on the table and then received an unmistakable urge: Leave it on the unmade bed - open. I'd never done such a thing before. Yet somehow it felt right, almost familiar.

I left the motel room with some hand luggage ahead of Gene.

When Gene joined me, I was startled to see tears in his eyes. He was so moved he couldn't speak. We both sat silent in the car for a moment, then he said, "That's something Phyllis did in every motel we ever stayed in - a witness to whoever cleaned the room."

As we headed west on Interstate 40, I felt just a little bit like a minister's wife.

LILLIAN LAYTON'S DAUGHTER

MYRTLE "COOKIE" POTTER

The minister approached me after church. "We're going to check in with people who haven't been here for a while to make sure that they're okay and let them know they're missed. Will you help?"

It was the tenth anniversary of my mother's death, and visiting strangers was the last thing I wanted to do. "Not today," I said. "I'm sorry." As I left the church, I prayed, "Lord, I'd give anything to feel Mama near again."

For years after Mama died, I had met with her friends to laugh and talk, remembering Mama's cheerful ways, her parties and how she made time to visit the housebound.

The word *visit* stung my conscience. I went back to the minister. "I'll help after all," I said, and he handed me a name and address.

When I drove to the house, a woman answered the door.

"I'm here to see Cora Heinecke," I said, introducing myself.

"Cora's in bed," the woman replied. "She's one-hundred years old, you know. But she loves company."

She led me to a dark bedroom, where she raised the shades and told Cora, "You have a visitor. Mrs Potter is from the church."

Cora sat up. "Lillian Layton's daughter?" she asked, "What a blessing!"

I looked at her, unbelieving. It turned out that Cora had been a close friend of my mother's!" For more than an hour we talked about Mama.

It was a discovery I never have forgotten: when I reached out to others, Mama came nearer to me.

Glorious Wonders

When my heart is overwhelmed:
lead me to the rock that is higher than I.

Psalm 61:2

Release Me

Lloyd B. Wilhide

"Ask and it shall be given you," Jesus said. I've always believed this, but never so much as the day of the accident in 1978.

At the time, I was seventy-five years old. The grass on our 121-acre dairy farm needed cutting, so I hitched a set of mower blades to my tractor and went to work. For added traction on our up-and-down terrain, I filled the tractor's rear wheels with 500 pounds of fluid. A 200-pound weight hung from each hub.

When I finished the job, I was on a light uphill grade near our chicken house. I switched off the ignition and climbed down from the high seat of the huge tractor. I was unfastening the mower blades when the tractor started moving backward.

I tried to twist around and jump on the seat, but I couldn't make it. The tractor's draw-bar hit me in the knees and knocked me flat, and the 700-pound left wheel rolled over my chest and stopped on top of it. I struggled for breath. The pain was agonising. I knew I was facing death, and I made my request.

"Please, God," I begged, "release me."

At that moment the tractor moved. It moved enough to free my chest and - to my astonishment - it moved uphill!

My dog, and then a farmhand, found me; and after six broken

ribs, two fractures, and twelve days in the hospital, I was back home, talking with the Maryland state trooper called to investigate the accident. "I won't try to explain it officially," he told me. "Why, a dozen men couldn't have moved that tractor off you."

Twelve men or twelve hundred men, it didn't matter. Asking God's help did.

RADIO RESCUE

THOMAS COVERDALE

Vietnam, December 14, 1967 - just before the first Tet Offensive. I was with Charlie Company, First Battalion, 25th Lightning Division, near Saigon. In the afternoon, a Vietcong death squad hit us, leaving ten dead. At sundown, feeling jittery, I went on patrol. Gribbit, Vigor, and I set up a listening post about 500 metres from camp. At 1.00am, I reported in: "This is Charlie, L.P. One. Lots of movement out here."

The radio crackled: "Get down! We're going to fire."

Our guys started throwing rockets into the bush; the enemy started their own barrage. We were pinned down. "Oh, God! Get us out of here ... please!" I prayed as I chewed dirt.

There was a thud, like someone punching my back. A grenade exploded. I felt blood trickling down my back. "We've been hit," I radioed, "we're coming in!" In spite of our wounds, we scrambled in the darkness through a field of mines and bales of razor-sharp wire. We stumbled into the arms of arriving medics.

Three weeks later, when all three of us were out of the hospital and back at camp, my platoon sergeant called me in. "Coverdale, how did you guys manage to let the medics know you'd been hit?"

"Radio, sir." I was surprised he should ask.

"Not with this, soldier," he replied, holding up a twisted, blackened box. It was the radio I had carried on my back. It had taken the full blast of the grenade, probably saving my life. And in doing so, the batteries, the crystal - every component - had been destroyed.

How did the medics get my SOS call? I don't know. But God does.

A Valuable Dream

Mary LaMagna Rocco

I suppose none of us know the meaning of dreams. But I know what prayers can do.

I was working the three-to-eleven shift at Miners Hospital in Spangler, Pennsylvania, when a patient I was feeding asked, "Why don't you have a little pin on like the other nurses?"

"I do," I said, reaching to show him the golden, wreath-shaped R.N. pin on my collar - one of my proudest possessions. It had been given to me when I graduated from nursing school in Altoona, and it stood for years of hard work and study. But now, when I looked down, the pin was gone.

I knew I had pinned it to my uniform just before I left the house. I looked everywhere for it. A colleague and I searched through all the linens and bedside equipment but found nothing. I even took a mop and dusted under the beds. At home, I turned the place upside down. No pin. Of course I could replace it, but a substitute would never mean as much. That night, as I lay in bed, I prayed that the Lord would help me find it.

Soon I was asleep. In the deep of night I had a dream. I dreamed that I got out of bed, put on my duster and slippers, and ran downstairs and out the door to a puddle of water in front of the house. And in this puddle was my pin.

The next morning I awoke disappointed. "It was only a worthless dream," I muttered. But as my head cleared, I seemed to hear a voice saying, "No, it's more than a dream. Go. See."

I put on my duster and slippers and walked out to the road in front of our house, and there I found a puddle of water. I placed my hand into the brown water. In a moment I felt in my hand an answered prayer.

A Fortuitous Phone Call

Mary Anne Hulford

I work for a large community hospital, placing patients in nursing homes. Of all my patients, the most difficult to place was Irene Manion.

No one from any social agency knew her. No one from a church claimed her. She had no relatives, no visitors, and apparently no friends. And she required a great deal of medical care.

For months I made hundreds of phone calls to nursing homes, trying to get her admitted. No one would accept her. I became obsessed with finding Irene a home. As I prayed to God each morning before work, I mentioned Irene Manion's name.

One day, after an arrangement that had looked hopeful fell through, I just sat at my desk and cried. Staring at Irene's thick, worn, faded paperwork, I said, "God, I give You Irene. Please place her where she'll get the best of care." I was really giving up.

A few minutes later I was back, dialling a nursing home I had called many, many times before. The admissions person wasn't there, and then, before I knew it, the operator connected me to a hallway wall phone. An evening nurse answered. In my frustration, I told her about my problem.

"What is the patient's name?" the nurse asked.

"Irene Manion," I told her.

To my amazement, the nurse said, "Send her to us in the morning. I'll arrange everything. She'll get the best of care."

The nurse then told me how, when her mother had died, she'd been raised by a neighbour, a woman she called "Mom." Now, after twelve years of desperately looking for that woman, her search had ended.

Irene Manion was her beloved "Mom."

The Name on the Mailbox

Virginia Cottrell

"Be bold, mighty forces will come to your aid." That's an adage I've long believed in. But there was a moment in my life that led me to believe that if you're sometimes struggling, mysterious forces will come to your aid.

At that time, when my family was struggling, I sought a job with Oklahoma's Department of Human Services. This was a bold move, for I had no diploma, having dropped out of school to marry. But eventually I passed the test and got the job.

My assignment was to locate and assist needy families, and locating them was often difficult. This particular day ten years ago, I'd heard of a needy family (no father, little money or food, frightened mother and children) living near Lake Texoma. This was dangerous country, but I felt it was my duty to find them. I drove all morning with little to guide me; in this gun-crazy backcountry you didn't just knock on any door and ask for directions.

Finally, in the early afternoon, I parked in the shade of a cottonwood tree and began to pray, asking God to direct me. I then looked down the lane I'd already driven down twice, and there was a lone mailbox plainly emblazoned with the family's name.

My visit went well; we'd be able to help this family with food and clothing. As I was leaving, the grateful mother marvelled that I'd found her house. "It wasn't hard," I said, "once I saw your name on the mailbox."

"My name?" the woman said to me, obviously mystified.

And going back to the road, I examined the mailbox again. There was no name. No name at all.

A Saving Sign

Dorothy Nicholas

We were sitting at the table in our Florida home and talking to our next door neighbours. This young couple had helped us a lot in the last year and a half, after my stroke and my husband's leg injury.

Unexpectedly, the husband began telling us the story of his troubled past. At age sixteen he'd fallen in with the wrong crowd in his hometown of Greenwood, South Carolina, and he had spent a year in a reformatory school. When he was released he'd had good intentions, but because of his record, he couldn't find a job.

He became desperate and decided to rob a local service station to get enough money to leave the state. He stole his father's car and gun, and just before closing time, he drove up to the service window of a gas station. He was about to demand all the money from the woman manager.

"Just then," he explained, "I looked up and saw the sign overhead. It read, 'God is Our Security Guard - Always on the Job.' And I knew I couldn't rob that place. I then rushed home and prayed all night. I was determined to get my life straightened out. And with God's help, I did."

As he finished, I looked at my husband. Both of us remembered a night thirteen years ago when I sat at our kitchen table in the same town of Greenwood, South Carolina, trying to make a sign for our business. I had scribbled down several words. Then finally it came to me, the slogan that my husband put on the sign that stood on the roof of the small service station that we managed:

God is our Security Guard - Always on the Job.

Her Cry of Glory

Jeanne M. Dams

The hospital chaplain sat by the dying woman's bed in the hospice ward. He knew little about her, except that the end was near. She had fought bravely, but after her last operation the doctors said there was little that could be done. Now she was unconscious, and although he could not speak with her, he tried to find the right words of prayer.

Her bed was cranked up and she was half sitting in order to make it easier for her to breathe through a tube in her throat.

Her breaths came harshly and slowly, but their rhythm was even. In the warm room, the chaplain felt tired and closed his eyes for a minute.

Suddenly he was started awake by a loud cry from the bed. The woman was sitting bolt upright. "My God!" she cried out.

The chaplain rose quickly to summon a nurse. But just then the woman sank back against the pillows, her eyes closed, a look of radiance on her face.

A nurse rushed in. "Did you call out?" she asked the chaplain as she took the woman's pulse. Quickly the nurse summed up the situation. "I'm afraid she's gone."

"No, I didn't speak," the chaplain said in wonderment, still thinking of the woman's ecstatic expression. "She did. She cried out, 'My God!'"

The nurse turned to him, puzzled. "But she couldn't have. Didn't you know? She had cancer of the larynx. Her voice box was destroyed weeks ago. She couldn't have said a word."

The Correct Phone Number

Edith M. Dean

My husband, Jim, and I were getting ready for bed when the phone rang. The stranger explained that she was Grace Morrison's aunt, "calling from Nebraska," and Grace's brother had been seriously injured in a car accident. No one knew how to get in touch with Grace. Did I?

Grace and I had once been office friends, but we hadn't spoken in years.

"I'm sorry," I said after fumbling through my address book, "I don't have Grace's address or phone number. Let me call you back if I find it."

"No, I'll call you in the morning," the woman said.

The memory of that pleading voice kept me up for hours looking through old files and address books. When I went to bed, I prayed and then tossed and turned, thinking of phone numbers in my sleep. When I woke up, my favourite pen was lying on the nightstand. I had no idea how it got there.

I left early for work that morning; when I came home, Jim exclaimed, "Thanks to you, Grace Morrison is on her way to Nebraska."

"Thanks to me?" I asked.

Jim looked at me, puzzled. "Yes. When her aunt called, I gave her the number you had written on that pad on the nightstand. Then she called back to say all was well."

"But, Jim," I said, "I never found it."

"Look," he said, handing me the pad. There in my handwriting was the correct phone number for Grace Morrison.

I sat down, mystified. And only then did I wonder: how did the aunt find me?

A Field of Cows

Elly Derr

Years ago, my husband, Dan, was a missionary pilot in Ecuador. We lived at the foot of the Andes Mountains; and when he flew, he kept in touch with me at the base camp by radio. One day I was logging his position and altitude when he announced that his Cessna had engine trouble. He needed to make an emergency landing.

I looked at my map and saw nothing but steep hills that dropped off into deep precipices. There was no flat space for miles around. From the sky, Dan searched for a road, a field, a meadow - any place he could possibly bring down the plane. He was losing altitude fast.

"Pray," he said to his passenger, a missionary travelling with her four children. "Pray," he said to me over the radio.

As the plane came through a pass, Dan saw a mountain village and a small green field. Down he came for a landing. He radioed his position to me, and I drove to meet him. When I arrived, Dan's plane was in a field surrounded by a crowd of Indians. My husband and his relieved passengers were unharmed. "*Es un milagro*," one farmer repeated over and over again. "It's a miracle."

I assumed he was talking about the plane's safe landing, but he had another *milagro* in mind.

That small green field had been filled with cows peacefully grazing. Suddenly, for no apparent reason, they had all started moving to one side of the field - just before Dan's plane came into view.

A Stunning Blue-White Light

Charles Kaelin, Jr., M.D.

We had been caught in a blizzard, and I was in a caravan going down a winding, snow-packed mountain highway near Lake Tahoe, Nevada. My wife and three children were in someone else's car.

Because of a malfunction, our van's lights, radio, wipers, heater, and windows no longer worked. Snow whirled through an open window. My body ached from the cold. Then the windshield became a white wall. I tried to lean out and sweep off the blinding snow with my arm. But it was no use.

Straining to see, I pulled onto the shoulder of the highway. The van lurched as a front wheel thudded against what felt like a boulder. I hit the brakes. When I jumped out, I found myself looking down into a white abyss; I'd almost driven over the edge!

"Jesus," I cried as I got back into the van, "I need your help."

Another driver stopped and got out of his car to direct me. I put the van in reverse. Just then a stunning blue-white light shot through the windshield and struck the steering wheel. I pressed my back into the seat as the flash raced through the steering column. In that instant, radio, lights, windows, wipers, heater - everything started working at once!

"Did you see that?" the other driver said.

At the bottom of the mountain, our family was reunited. People have told me the strange flash might have been snow lightning. For me, it was the answer to a prayer.

The Phone that Worked

Orpha E. Abesamis

Mother and I anxiously watched the news about the summer storm that had hit back in our native Philippines. We tried calling my sister, Ruth, who lived alone, more than an hour's drive from the rest of our family there. But the storm had knocked out her phone.

Ruth planned to join us in Philadelphia after her immigration papers were approved. Mother, eighty-two and suffering from heart problems, would not rest easy until Ruth was with us again.

One week later, word got through that Ruth's visa had been granted. Her phone was still out, but she would call us to make arrangements as soon as possible. Mother was cheered by the news. But when she gasped for air, I knew her condition was worsening.

Mother's doctor scheduled surgery. And he prepared me for the worst: Mother might not survive.

"God," I prayed, "if only I could get through to Ruth . . ."

A strange impulse seized me. Call her. I knew Ruth would have called if she could, but I decided to try anyway. As I finished dialling, I anticipated static on the other end. The phone rang.

"Hello," Ruth said clearly.

She took the next plane, and we had a joyful reunion in the

hospital as Ruth talked about home. The day after surgery, Mother slipped into God's presence.

"I wouldn't have reached you in time," I said to Ruth, "if your phone hadn't been working."

"But it wasn't," she said. "Right after we talked, it went dead again."

A Bible Found

Charles Sweitzer

When I entered the service during World War II, I was given a small, pocket-size New Testament with my name inscribed on the inside front cover. Often I read passages for comfort from the stresses of Army life. But just before the invasion of Europe, we were told we weren't allowed to have any personal identification with us other than our dog tags. Reluctantly I handed in my Bible.

I made my way safely through Normandy, then moved with the American troops across France into Holland, Belgium, and Germany. I often thought of my Bible, and when I prayed, I could still remember God's promises written there.

At the war's end, I returned to the States. Eventually I married and raised a family. One day in 1994, my daughter Nancy called me; she and her Danish husband, Jorgen, had been unpacking after a recent move.

"One box was full of books," she said. "But I couldn't read a word of them because they were all written in Danish. So I asked Jorgen to look at them. He said they were hymnals he had bought ten years ago at an estate sale in Denmark.

"Jorgen sorted through the books, pulled out one and said, 'Here, this one's in English." You'll never guess what it was!" Nancy exclaimed. "On the inside cover was your name, Dad."

For fifty years I had been separated from my pocket-sized Bible. To my delight it had come back to me.

The Unseen Photographer

Kathy Pierce

I meant to set the alarm for dawn that third night in Israel with my church group. I wanted to get up with the sun and say my daily prayers, as I always did at home. I especially wanted to pray while the sun rose over the Sea of Galilee - the very sea where Jesus sailed - and take a snapshot. I put my camera on the nightstand, then rested my eyes.

Only for a second, I promised myself, then I'll set the alarm . . .

The next thing I knew, sunlight filled my room. It was morning! How could I have let this happen?

I jumped out of bed and from the balcony looked at the fat sun hovering above the sea. That had been our last night in Galilee. I'll never see the sunrise here, I thought.

The rest of the trip through the Holy Land went well. I shot rolls and rolls of film, but in the back of my mind, I was frustrated. The picture I wanted most would never be.

When I got home I developed nearly 300 photographs. One was of a glorious sunrise over the Sea of Galilee. That's odd, I thought. I could only guess that my hotel roommate, Kitty, had taken the picture with my camera and wanted to surprise me.

At our tour group's reunion several weeks later, I showed her the snapshot. "Thanks, Kitty," I said.

She looked bewildered. "I didn't take that," she told me.

I asked around the group if anyone had taken a picture with my camera. No one had, but Someone had made sure I got the shot I wanted.

Sam, AKA Gus

Nancy Rose

My husband has a soft spot for strays. Driving down the highway one rainy day, we spotted a hulking mass of greyish-black fur with paws the size of a bear's, wondering along the roadside. "We already have two dogs and two cats," I protested as he pulled over.

"We can't just leave him here," he said. "No telling what will happen to him." He opened the door and the dog climbed in.

"Okay," I agreed, "but we have to try hard to find his owner." The dog seemed friendly enough, but there was a look about him that spoke of a wilder nature.

We called him Gus, and we ran ads in the paper and on the radio, but no one claimed him. For the next year and a half, Gus lived with us. He was a boisterous dog, and one day his energy got the best of him and he nipped someone.

A dog his size needed more space to run. "Lord, help us find the home where Gus will be happy," I prayed.

We started a new search, for a new owner, a home where Gus was meant to be. One day a friend mentioned a family that might be interested. "They used to have a big dog out on their farm. The boys were really torn up when Sam disappeared," he said.

Two days later the Delancy family came to meet Gus. The kids piled out of the car. "Sam!" they cried, as the dog, tail wagging, bounded toward them joyously. "We thought you'd never come back!"

Sam, AKA Gus, was the happiest dog in the world. He was going home at last.

ELIZABETH'S CARD

JILL RENICH-MEYERS

My husband, Fred, had passed away suddenly. I was grief stricken. I prayed for something - anything - to hang onto.

One dark day I felt especially alone. I walked out to get the mail, opened the box, and found a card from my friend Elizabeth. She had lost her husband six months earlier.

How is she managing? I wondered as I ripped open the envelope. Inside the card, across from the printed message, she had written an ink in her distinctive hand, "It does get easier."

Her words lessened my despair a little. God, if your healing is there for Elizabeth, it must be there for me too.

To try to get my mind off things, I started cleaning the house. While dusting behind Fred's desk, I found the shoes he had bought the week before he died. Fred will never walk with me again, I thought, tears forming in my eyes. Then, softly, Elizabeth's message came to mind. I opened her card. It does get easier. I wiped away my tears and continued my chores.

During the next several months, with the help of family, friends, and prayer, things did get easier. But nothing meant more to me than Elizabeth's words.

Months later I took out Elizabeth's cards again. I wanted to drop her a line. When I opened the card I couldn't believe my eyes. There was no handwritten message. No personal writing at all except for her signature. God had transferred his comforting words form her card to my heart.

A Silver Case

Dina Donohue

India Albery was, perhaps, the most unusual person ever to work at Guideposts. Lady Albery - for that was her title - seldom spoke about herself. We knew only that she had come from England and her early life had been privileged, but that when she came to Guideposts, she was old and alone and impoverished, living in a shabby room with few cherished keepsakes.

She met adversity bravely, but with a stern and haughty demeanour. I tried hard, but I could not break through her British reserve. I used to pray that I would find some way to reach her, but she was too proud to let any emotion show.

One lunch hour in December, I was browsing in an antique shop, a favourite pastime. I seldom purchased anything, but this day was different. I spied an enamel pencil in a silver case. It had a large "A" in its elaborate monogram, and I felt an urging - almost a physical nudge - to buy it for Lady Albery.

"What's this?" she asked brusquely when I handed her the tiny package.

"Just a little Christmas something," I said apprehensively.

When Lady Albery opened the package and saw the silver case, her body tensed and her eyes filled with tears. "Dina," she said -

never before had she used my first name - "Dina, how did you know?"

"Know what?" I asked.

"This once belonged to me," she said. "I had to sell it years ago when I was hungry and desperate. It was given to me by someone I loved. And now your kindness has brought it back."

A circle of love, I thought. I've been part of a circle of love.

And Lady Albery never forgot it.

Also in the TRUE STORIES series

STORIES OF FRIENDSHIP

INTRODUCED BY

BRIAN GREENAWAY

A CELEBRATION OF THE JOYS AND RICHES OF FRIENDSHIP: THE SMALL ACTS OF KINDNESS, THE LAUGHTER, THE TEARS, THE MEMORIES THAT ONLY THE ENDURING BOND OF FRIENDSHIP PROVIDES.

Enjoy the 'best of the best': a collection of true, heart-warming, inspiring and uplifting stories of friendship, all carefully selected from Guideposts magazine, known for its captivating real-life stories.

STORIES OF FRIENDSHIP features over fifty heart-warming anecdotes and stories.

- Enjoy reflections on the meaning of friendship, as in Ralph Waldo Emerson's homage to friends old and new
- Reflect on stories of kindness, as seen in Dennis Mathis' tale of renovating a house for a neighbour in need
- Warm to stories on the lasting nature of friendship, as in Pamela Kennedy's 'Long Distance Friends'
- Relive the rich memories that friendship provides, as retold by Marjorie Holmes

Discover the lasting peace and comfort provided by Jesus, the greatest friend of all.

Eagle
ISBN 0 86347 605 8

Also in the TRUE STORIES series

STORIES OF COMFORT

BY CORRIE TEN BOOM, MARJORIE HOLMES, PAMELA KENNEDY, NORMAN VINCENT PEALE AND OTHERS

COLLECTED HERE ARE STORIES OF HOPE AND COMFORT BY MANY WHO HAVE EXPERIENCED DIFFICULTIES, CHALLENGES AND SORROWS, BUT IN THEIR OWN WAY HAVE OVERCOME. THE AUTHORS OF THESE UP-LIFTING ACCOUNTS HAVE OFTEN BEEN SURPRISED BY THE HOPE THAT CAN SPRING, SOMETIMES UNEXPECTEDLY, FROM EVEN THE DARKEST SITUATIONS.

STORIES OF COMFORT will encourage and inspire with its accounts of the journey of grief, sorrow and fear to peace, hope and faith. It features over fifty heart-warming and inspiring stories. All of them are true and contributors include many unsung heroes, as well as names you will recognise, such as Corrie Ten Boom, Marjorie Holmes, Pamela Kennedy and Norman Vincent Peale among others.

Eagle
ISBN 0 86347 616 3

Also in the TRUE STORIES series

MIRACLES OF HEALING

INTRODUCED BY

JENNIFER REES LARCOMBE

DURING HIS EARTHLY MINISTRY JESUS CHRIST HEALED MANY PEOPLE – ORDINARY PEOPLE – SOME WITH MUCH FAITH AND SOME WITH ONLY A LITTLE.

Today, all over the world people of vastly different backgrounds are still being healed by God. Gathered together here are the 'best-of-the-best' of remarkable true stories selected from Guideposts magazine, known for its captivating real-life stories.

These honest stories of physical, emotional, spiritual and psychological healing are recounted in the words of those who experienced or witnessed a miracle. Some are dramatic and awe-inspiring, others are a series of 'God-incidences', but all reveal the mercy and goodness of a God who hears our prayers.

Eagle
ISBN 0 86347 604 X

WALKING WITH GOD

MARTIN MANSER
AND
MIKE BEAUMONT

365 PROMISES AND PRAYERS FROM THE BIBLE FOR EVERY DAY OF THE YEAR

A mere plane journey sometimes has its turbulent moments; life too can have its ups and downs. This book has been written out of an absolute conviction that God is with us always, and that his presence can be experienced particularly in such times. God does not want us to separate our spiritual lives from the rest of our life, but to remember he is with us in those times of illness, hardship, bereavement or difficulty – and of course, to know the same in life's joys!

WALKING WITH GOD takes promises and prayers from the Bible as its daily foundation. The aim is simply to help you meet with God daily! He is the God of the promises. He is the God who inspires our prayers. He is the one we can turn to in every situation in life: when we are puzzled, when we find it difficult to carry on, when we need guidance and help, and when we are just simply grateful.

Each day's reading begins with an opening verse from the Bible, which is then considered and applied, and closes with a final Bible verse. Sometimes other Bible extracts are quoted, and every book in the Bible is drawn from over the course of the year, encouraging us to turn to God in every situation in life.

If possible, find a quiet place where you can let go of the busyness of life for a few moments and quieten your spirit to be still, to listen and talk to God as you think over and pray about each day's reading.

Eagle
ISBN 0 86347 627 9